Road to the
RESURRECTION
Explore and Share the Miracle of Easter

A publication of

Riverside, California
www.harvest.org

Greg Laurie is senior pastor of Harvest Christian Fellowship in Riverside, California.

Road to the Resurrection: Explore and Share the Miracle of Easter

Text Copyright © 2011, 2004 by Greg Laurie and Harvest Ministries.
All rights reserved.

Portions adapted from:
© 2004 The Passion of the Christ: A Biblical Guide
© 2004 The Resurrection of the Christ: A Biblical Guide

Design: Harvest Design
Copywriting: Harvest Publications
Copyediting: Harvest Publications
Research: Harvest Publications

Printed in the United States of America.

ISBN-13: 978-1-61754-021-9

TABLE OF CONTENTS

PREFACE

"He is Risen!"

These words are a traditional greeting among Christians on Easter Day, and they are answered with the joyful countersign, "He is risen indeed!"

But much more than a happy greeting, these words express the foundational truth upon which all of Christianity hinges. As the Apostle Paul said, "If Christ is not risen, then our preaching is empty and your faith is also empty" (1 Corinthians 15:14).

But Christ is risen…He is risen indeed! We, as Christians, therefore have more reason to rejoice, more reason to celebrate, and more reason to share our Good News than anyone else on earth.

In conjunction with this book, we are offering special bonus material to help you explore the miracle of Easter, and to share it with others. This material includes special music, videos, devotional messages, and more. To access this material, we invite you to visit

risen.harvest.org

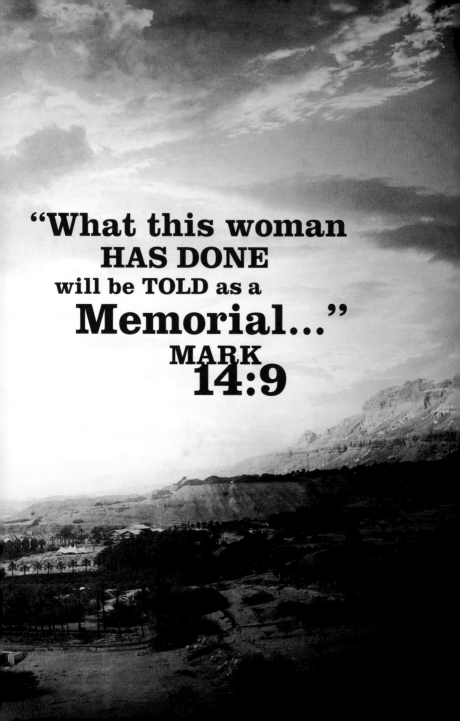

CHAPTER 1

THE HEART OF EASTER

"A lifetime of love poured out in the space of a few hours"

In the Gospels we read that Jesus clearly and repeatedly told his disciples what was coming. The Road to the Resurrection was mapped out for them in plain and definite terms. In fact, in Luke 18:31–33 NLT we read,

> Taking the twelve disciples aside, Jesus said, "Listen, we're going up to Jerusalem, where all the predictions of the prophets concerning the Son of Man will come true. He will be handed over to the Romans, and He will be mocked, treated shamefully, and spit upon. They will flog Him with a whip and kill Him, but on the third day He will rise again."

Jesus wasn't mincing words. There's no ambiguity in His statement. Nothing complex or cryptic or convoluted. But despite the simplicity and candor of His words, verse 34 tells us,

> But they didn't understand any of this. The significance of His words was hidden from them, and they failed to grasp what He was talking about.

The importance of Easter went right over their heads. And the same is often true today. So many people just don't "get" the significance of Easter. It is garbled in their minds with egg hunts, plastic grass, new dresses, bunnies, chicks, or chocolate. So what is it really all about?

> Jesus was in Bethany at the home of Simon, a man who had previously had leprosy. While He was eating, a woman came in with a beautiful alabaster jar of expensive perfume made from essence of nard. She broke open the jar and poured the perfume over his head. Some of those at the table were indignant. "Why waste such expensive perfume?" they asked. "It could have been sold for a year's wages and the money given to the poor!" So they scolded her harshly. But Jesus replied, "Leave her alone. Why criticize her for doing such a good thing to Me? You will always have the poor among you, and you can help them whenever you want to. But you will not always have Me. She has done what she could and has anointed My body for burial ahead of time. I tell you the truth, wherever the Good News is preached throughout the world, this woman's deed will be remembered and discussed" (Mark 14:3–9).

This woman was listening. She allowed His words to penetrate her mind and to break her heart. That broken heart led to a broken jar, and the fragrance of her worship filled the house.

We are told that her gift was worth a year's wages. That is an amazing sacrifice—a whole year's worth of work poured out in the space of a few seconds. But it is apparent that this woman measured its value against the forthcoming sacrifice of her Savior—a lifetime of love poured out in the space of a few hours, on the cross. That is what Easter is about—the love of God. A love that endured pain, ridicule, anguish, and death for the sake of you and me. And what should be our response? Worship. Pure and unadulterated worship.

This Easter, allow the words of Jesus to penetrate your mind. And allow the magnitude of His suffering to break your heart, so that the fragrance of your worship can be poured out upon the Savior.

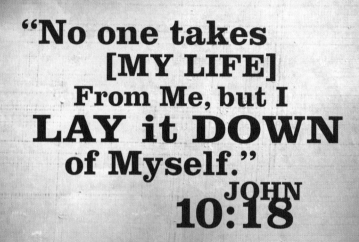

"No one takes [MY LIFE] From Me, but I **LAY it DOWN** of Myself."

JOHN 10:18

CHAPTER 2

WHY CHRIST HAD TO DIE

"Christ suffered and died on the cross for numerous reasons. But the simplest reason is He loved us."

Ever since I was a small child, I have always had a great admiration for the historical person known as Jesus Christ. I had seen the movies Hollywood had made about His life. But the one thing I didn't like about the story of Jesus was how it ended. I used to think, *Whoever wrote the story of Jesus ought to rewrite it again with a happier ending. This whole story of His crucifixion should be edited out. It's just not the way His life should have ended.* You may understand why I would think such a thing. It seemed to me that Jesus was on something of a roll, after all. He was healing and teaching people. Little children were flocking to Him. Clearly, His popularity was growing by leaps and bounds. But then the unexpected occurred. Jesus was murdered. It is no wonder some people think to themselves, *Why do they have to put Jesus on a cross and kill Him? What a tragic and unnecessary ending to such a wonderful life.*

Becoming a Christian radically transformed my opinion on the ending of Jesus Christ's story. After reading the Gospel accounts for the first time in my life, I began to see that the crucifixion of Jesus was really the primary reason He came to this earth in the first place. The crucifixion does not read like a storybook ending, because it does not come from the pages of a storybook. It is no mere fairytale. It is a historically true, real-life story, recorded in the pages of Scripture. And the Bible gives us real-life reasons Jesus had to die on the cross. Christ suffered and died on the cross for numerous reasons. But the simplest reason is He loved us. The Apostle John said it well when he wrote, "In this is love, not that we loved God, but that He loved us and sent His Son to be the propitiation for our sins." (1 John 4:10). God's love for us and His desire to make right our relationship with Him was why Jesus humbled Himself by becoming a man and dying on the cross for our sins (see Philippians 2:5–11).

To demonstrate the passion behind Christ's love, here are four reasons He died on the cross:

- To bring us into a right relationship with God (see Colossians 1:19–20; 2 Corinthians 5:18). Our sin had separated us from God. In order to restore our relationship with God, He sent His Son, Jesus Christ, to pay the penalty for our sins. That penalty was the cross. With the death and resurrection of Christ, we can now have that right and holy relationship with God by grace through faith in Jesus Christ (see Ephesians 2:8–9).

- To forgive us of our sins and the guilt that accompanied them. In the Hebrew Scriptures, the shed blood of animals was symbolic of the forgiveness of sins. The Bible makes it clear that without this shedding of blood, we cannot be forgiven of our sins (see Hebrews 9:22). So Jesus came to die as a once-and-for-all sacrifice to forgive us of our sins and free us from guilt (see Acts 13:39).

- To satisfy the radical requirement of the holiness of God (see Leviticus 11:44). God's holiness made a penalty for sin necessary. God's love endured that penalty for the sinner and made payment of the penalty possible. Jesus paid that penalty by experiencing God's wrath and separation from Him on the cross (see Romans 5:9–10; Hebrews 10:12). Jesus was forsaken of God so we don't have to be. He was forsaken for a time that we might enjoy God's presence forever (see Matthew 27:46; see also Hebrews 10:12–14).

- To perform the righteous requirements of the law (see Matthew 3:15; 5:17; Galatians 4:4; 1 Corinthians 1:30). Jesus, through His holy life and suffering on the cross, lived the perfect life we were required to live and took the punishment that we deserved.

These are just some of the reasons Jesus Christ died. But the Apostle Paul summed up the message of the cross best when he wrote, "[Christ] died for us so that…we can live with him forever" (1 Thessalonians 5:10 NLT). Clearly, Jesus' death was no ridiculous ending. The cross did not ruin everything. Jesus' death and resurrection saved us from our ruin and gave us life everlasting. This is why we must not blame the people of that day for executing Jesus. Scripture provides no room for anti-Semitism and no room for hatred. Our sins put Him on that cross 2000 years ago. The death of Christ is part of the happiest story ever told. It is the story of how God became a man so He could die for our sins and so we could be friends with Him once again. He did it for you and He did it for me. All that is left up to us is to believe in Him (see Romans 3:22).

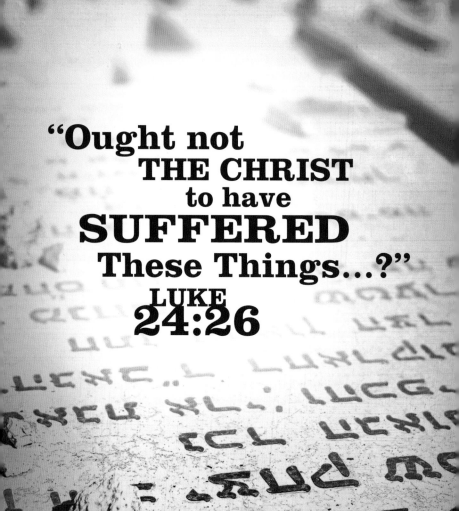

"Ought not
THE CHRIST
to have
SUFFERED
These Things...?"
LUKE
24:26

CHAPTER 3

THE SCRIPTURE SPEAKS

"Prophecy is a person of God speaking, proclaiming, or announcing a message under the influence of God's inspiration."

The word *prophecy* refers to the God-given message of the prophet. Prophets were people of God who experienced a special encounter with God, in which He would directly convey a message to them. Prophecy varied from messages of judgment, salvation, assurance, and sometimes future events. Whatever the content, prophecy is a person of God speaking, proclaiming, or announcing a message under the influence of God's inspiration. It is God's authoritative word to His people.

Included below are some of the prophecies that predicted the death of Christ, made hundreds of years before His crucifixion.

The Christ's Triumphal Entry
Prophesied: Zechariah 9:9
Fulfilled: Matthew 21:1–11; Mark 11:1–11;
Luke 19:28–40; John 12:12–19

In the Old Testament, the prophet Zechariah called attention to the long-awaited King, the Christ. This King is not like the many wicked kings Israel lived under. He is righteous and humble—so humble that He rides upon a donkey instead of a horse (an animal associated with warfare). All four Gospel writers record Jesus entering into Jerusalem on a donkey.

The Christ Would Be Betrayed by a Close Friend (Judas Iscariot)
Prophesied: Psalm 41:9
Fulfilled: Luke 22:47–48

Judas Iscariot was one of the twelve disciples whom Jesus Christ called to be close to Him. As the manager of the group's assets, Judas was known for pilfering money. Judas singled out Jesus with a kiss of betrayal in the Garden of Gethsemane.

The Christ Would Be Betrayed for Thirty Pieces of Silver
Prophesied: Zechariah 11:12–13
Fulfilled: Matthew 26:14–15

Just as the prophet Zechariah foretold, Judas Iscariot betrayed Jesus Christ to the religious leaders for 30 pieces of silver, the price of a slave in those days.

The Christ Would Be Scourged and Spat Upon
Prophesied: Isaiah 50:6
Fulfilled: Matthew 26:67; 27:26

Jesus Christ was spat upon—an act showing contempt and scorn. As punishment, Jesus' accusers beat Him with a "cat-o'-nine-tails," a whip that was made of cords fastened to a handle with bits of bone and/or metal attached to it.

The Christ's Blood Money Would Be Used to Buy a Potter's Field
Prophesied: Zechariah 11:12–13
Fulfilled: Matthew 27:9–10

Judas Iscariot, the betrayer, flung the "blood money" on the Temple floor after declaring he had betrayed innocent blood.

The high priests decided to use the money to buy a field, known as Potter's Field, to use as a burial place for strangers.

The Christ Would Be Crucified between Two Thieves
Prophesied: Isaiah 53:12
Fulfilled: Matthew 27:38, Mark 15:27–28, Luke 22:37

Two criminals were crucified at the same time as Jesus Christ, one on His right and one on His left.

The Christ Would Be Given Vinegar to Drink
Prophesied: Psalm 69:21
Fulfilled: Matthew 27:34, 48; John 19:28–30

After Christ said, "I thirst," He was offered wine to drink that was mingled with gall. This drink was used to numb pain. After tasting it, Jesus refused it, not wanting to take anything that would diminish the pain He came to experience for our sins.

The Christ Would Suffer the Piercing of His Hands and Feet
Prophesied: Psalm 22:16; Zechariah 12:10
Fulfilled: Mark 15:25, John 19:34, 37; 20:25–27

In Roman crucifixions, the victim's hands were nailed or bound to the cross with arms extended and raised up. The feet of the crucified were nailed with one or two spikes. Jesus Christ's accusers nailed both his hands and feet to the cross.

The Christ's Garments Would Be Divided and Gambled For
Prophesied: Psalm 22:18
Fulfilled: Luke 23:34; John 19:23–24

The Roman soldiers nearest the cross divided the garments of Jesus, except for His seamless tunic. They instead decided to cast lots to see who would get the whole garment.

The Christ Would Be Surrounded and Ridiculed by His Enemies
Prophesied: Psalm 22:7–8
Fulfilled: Matthew 27:39–44; Mark 15:29–32

The chief priests, scribes, elders, and people passing by all hurled abuse at Jesus Christ. Even the two criminals on the crosses were casting insults at Him before one of them put his faith in Him.

The Christ Would Thirst
Prophesied: Psalm 22:15
Fulfilled: John 19:28

Jesus displayed His humanity when he experienced physical needs on the cross. His deity did not lessen the horrific treatment brought upon Him as He suffered on the cross for humankind.

The Christ Would Commend His Spirit to the Father
Prophesied: Psalm 31:5
Fulfilled: Luke 23:46

Jesus Christ willingly committed Himself to His Father after He had finished all that was required for sinners to have forgiveness and removal of their sins.

The Christ's Bones Would Not Be Broken
Prophesied: Exodus 12:46; Numbers 9:12; Psalm 34:20
Fulfilled: John 19:33–36

Oftentimes to hasten the death of the crucified, the soldiers would break the legs of the victim so that suffocation would occur. Jesus was already dead when the soldiers came to perform this act on Him, so there was no need to break any of His bones.

The Christ Would Be Forsaken by God
Prophesied: Psalm 22:1
Fulfilled: Matthew 27:46

On the cross, Jesus Christ cried out, asking God why He had forsaken Him. Many believe it was at this time that fellowship was severed between God the Father and God the Son. The cause of this severed fellowship was the sin of the world falling upon Jesus as He paid the price for humanity's sin. Jesus revealed this separation of intimacy by using the name *God* instead of His more often used and more intimate term *Father*.

The Christ Would Be Raised from the Dead
Prophesied: Psalm 16:10
Fulfilled: Matthew 28:2–7

Long before Jesus was born in the little town of Bethlehem, it was prophesied that the Messiah would rise from the dead.

The Christ Would Ascend to Heaven
Prophesied: Psalm 24:7–10
Fulfilled: Mark 16:19; Luke 24:51; Acts 1:9

Forty days after His resurrection, Jesus Christ ascended to heaven to be with the Father.

The Christ Would Be Seated at the Father's Right Hand
Prophesied: Psalm 110:1
Fulfilled: Matthew 22:44; Hebrews 10:12–13

The right hand is a symbol of honor and strength, the supreme seat of authority. The Father exalted Jesus Christ to this place signifying that He fulfilled all that was required of Him.

JESUS CHRIST PREDICTS THE CRUCIFIXION AND RESURRECTION

Jesus made predictions concerning His own death, resurrection, ascension, and more.

First Prediction
Predicted: Matthew 16:21–28; Mark 8:31–39; Luke 9:21–34

Second Prediction
Predicted: Matthew 20:17–29; Mark 10:32–34; Luke 18:31–34

Third Prediction
Predicted: Matthew 26:2–5; Mark 14:1–9

Fulfilled: Matthew 27–28; Mark 15–16; Luke 23–24; John 19–20

Much to the surprise and dismay of the disciples, Jesus Christ predicted to them His soon coming suffering, death, and resurrection. He later fulfilled His words when He was crucified, buried, and raised from the dead on the third day.

CHRIST PREDICTS HIS POST-RESURRECTION MEETING WITH THE DISCIPLES IN GALILEE

Predicted: Matthew 26:32; Mark 14:28; 16:7
Fulfilled: Matthew 28:9–10, 16–20; John 20:19–29; 21:1–15

The Risen Christ met with His disciples in Galilee in order to give hope to His dismayed followers, prove He had risen bodily, and commission them to make disciples of all the nations.

CHRIST PREDICTS THE ASCENSION

Predicted: John 1:50–51; 7:33–34; 8:14; 20:17
Fulfilled: Mark 16:19, Luke 24:51, Acts 1:9

The word *ascension* simply means the act of going upward. To speak of "the Ascension" signifies Christ's glorification at the right hand of God and the hope for believers that they too will one day ascend into heaven.

CHRIST PREDICTS THE DAY OF PENTECOST

Predicted: John 7:37–39; 15:26–27; 16:7; Acts 1:4–5
Fulfilled: Acts 2:1–4

Pentecost, or Feast of Weeks (see Exodus 34:22; Deuteronomy 16:10), was a Jewish festival celebrated seven weeks after Passover. In the New Testament, Pentecost was the day God empowered the first Christians with the Holy Spirit (see Acts 2).

CHRIST PREDICTS THE BIRTH OF THE CHURCH

Predicted: Matthew 16:18–19
Fulfilled: Acts 2

On Pentecost, the first-century believers were empowered with the Holy Spirit (see Acts 2). This endowed them (and all Christians) with spiritual gifts that enabled them to carry on God's mission and purpose through the collective body of believers known as "the church."

"For GOD so **LOVED** The World..." JOHN 3:16

CHAPTER 4

THE PEOPLE, PLACES, AND CHRONOLOGY OF THE CROSS

"The hour has come that the Son of Man should be glorified."
—John 12:23

Andrew

The brother of Simon Peter, Andrew was a disciple of John the Baptist and was the first of the apostles to be called by Jesus Christ (see John 1:35–42). In the events following the Resurrection, Andrew was among the apostles who were present at the Mount of Olives to witness the ascension of Jesus Christ (see Acts 1:9–13).

Annas, the Former High Priest

Annas was a former high priest (A.D. 6–15) and father-in-law to Joseph Caiaphas, the high priest during the time of Christ. The Gospels continue to refer to Annas as high priest due to his continued power after his official term in office. In a gesture of respect and acknowledgment of Annas' influence, Caiaphas had Annas begin the preliminary hearings of Christ (see John 18:13). It was there that Annas questioned Christ and then sent Him bound to Caiaphas (see John 18:24). Ultimately, Annas was simply a political pawn, as his reputation added potential credibility to the unjust plot to kill Jesus Christ.

The Apostles

Also known as the "Twelve" and the "disciples," the apostles were men whom Jesus Christ called and sent out to preach the Good News of the kingdom of God.

1. Peter (Simon)
2. Andrew (Brother of Peter)
3. James (Son of Zebedee)
4. John (Brother of James)
5. Philip
6. Bartholomew (Nathanael)
7. Thomas
8. Matthew (or Levi, the Tax Collector)
9. James (Son of Alphaeus)
10. Judas, Son of James (Thaddaeus)
11. Simon (the Zealot)
12. Judas Iscariot (the Betrayer)

After Christ ascended into heaven, Matthias was chosen to replace Judas as the twelfth apostle of Jesus Christ (see Acts 1:16–26).

Barabbas

Barabbas was a known revolutionary convicted of murder during an insurrection in Jerusalem against the Roman and provincial Jewish government (see Luke 23:19).

Barabbas' only appearance in the life of the Christ was in Pontius Pilate's trial of Jesus Christ. It was there that Pilate tried to free Christ by the means of what is known as the Passover privilege, where the crowd was allowed the option of choosing one prisoner to be set free. When Pilate offered the option of releasing Jesus, the crowds shouted, "Kill Him, and release Barabbas to us!" (Luke 23:18 NLT). Pilate appeased the crowds and released Barabbas, leaving Jesus to be scourged and then crucified.

Bartholomew

One of the twelve apostles, Bartholomew was among those who
were present at the Mount of Olives to witness the ascension of
Jesus Christ (see Acts 1:9–13). Typically, Bartholomew is identified
as the disciple Nathanael.

Bethany

Bethany, a city located off of the Jericho road less than two miles
from Jerusalem, was positioned on the southeastern slopes of the
Mount of Olives. In his Gospel, Luke writes that the ascension of
Jesus Christ transpired in Bethany: "And He led them out as far
as Bethany, and He lifted up His hands and blessed them. Now it
came to pass, while He blessed them, that He was parted from them
and carried up into heaven." (24:50–51). In Acts, Luke places the
Ascension at the Mount of Olives (see Acts 1:6–12). This difference
in detail poses no significant problems since Bethany sat at the foot
of the Mount of Olives.

Cleopas

Luke 24:18 identifies Cleopas as one of the two disciples who
encountered the risen Christ on the road to Emmaus.

The Criminals on the Crosses

Jesus Christ was crucified with two criminals, one on His left side
and the other on His right side. One of these convicted criminals
joined Jesus' scoffers by saying, "If You are the Christ, save Yourself
and us." (Luke 23:39). Just then, the other criminal protested,
explaining that he and the other criminal deserved death for their
evil deeds, but Jesus, however, was innocent. This criminal then
looked to Jesus and said, "Lord, remember me when you come into
your kingdom." Jesus replied, "Assuredly, I say to you, today you will
be with Me in Paradise." (Luke 23:42–43).

The believing criminal is a testimony that forgiveness of sins
is not based on any work of our own, for he was a convicted
criminal—not a saint. Instead, our salvation is based on God's
grace through our faith in Him (see Ephesians 2:8–9).

The Empty Tomb

The Garden Tomb was the burial site of Jesus Christ. Unlike tombs today, this tomb was carved out of a rock with the entrance covered by a large stone. Luke, in his Gospel, tells us that it was a new tomb where no one had ever been laid (see Luke 23:53). All four Gospels record the female followers of Christ appearing at the tomb early Sunday morning, only to find it empty. It was there that the angel proclaimed the message of the Resurrection, and hope was restored to all of Christ's followers (see Matthew 28:1–10; Mark 16:1–8; Luke 24:1–7; John 20:1–17).

Emmaus

A village seven miles out of Jerusalem, Emmaus was the destination of two discouraged disciples, Cleopas and another unnamed disciple (see Luke 24:13–18). There on the Emmaus road, the two disciples encountered a stranger who asked them about their conversation concerning Jesus of Nazareth. The stranger was no other than the risen Lord. The two disciples were unable to recognize Jesus because God had kept them from realizing who He was.

While walking on the road, Jesus taught them everything that the writings of Moses and the prophets said concerning the Christ. Later that day, Cleopas and the other disciple begged Christ to stay the night with them because it was getting late (see Luke 24:29). When the three of them sat down to eat, Christ blessed the food and suddenly "their eyes were opened, and they recognized him" (see Luke 24:31). At that moment of discovery, Jesus disappeared!

Within the hour, the two witnesses of the risen Christ were traveling back to Jerusalem. Upon arrival in Jerusalem, they heard other accounts of the resurrected Lord and then reported to the Eleven their meeting with the risen Christ. Just then, Jesus appeared before the group, and showed them His nail-pierced hands and feet so they would know He was no ghost (see Luke 24:32–40). He had truly risen bodily from the dead.

Field of Blood (*Akeldama*)

Also known as "Potter's Field," the leading priests purchased this plot of land with the thirty pieces of silver that Judas Iscariot returned to them. The priests were not able to return the money to the Temple treasury because it had been used to pay for murder (see Matthew 27:1–10). Instead, they bought the Potter's Field with it and used it as a cemetery for foreigners.

The First Century Temple (19 B.C.–A.D. 70)

The Jerusalem Temple was the center of religious and social life for the Jews of Christ's day. Herod the Great built the Temple in order to appease the Jews and build a structure that would rival Solomon's Temple, which King Nebuchadnezzar burned in 587 B.C. The Temple was an ornate house of worship that filled an area measuring approximately 490 yards from north to south and 325 yards from east to west. The main construction of the Temple was finished in 9 B.C. with the final construction ending in A.D. 64. Almost seven years later, the Romans utterly annihilated the Herodian Temple.

Significant events occurred there, such as Jesus' cleansing of the moneychangers and His preaching about the coming destruction of the Temple. In his Gospel, Luke writes that after Jesus ascended into heaven, the disciples went to Jerusalem "and were continually in the temple praising and blessing God." (Luke 24:53). Once the Holy Spirit came upon the believers, the Book of Acts says that they worshiped together at the Temple each day, all the while praising God (see 2:46, 47).

Galilee

The location of Jesus Christ's childhood (Nazareth is in lower Galilee), Galilee was the primary setting of Jesus' ministry. He taught ten of His thirty-two recorded parables in Galilee and performed twenty-five of His thirty-three recorded miracles there. Jesus recognized that the major centers of Galilee were not accepting the gospel, so He denounced such Galilean cities as Korazin,

Bethsaida, and Capernaum (see Matthew 11:21–24). He and His disciples then began proclaiming the Good News of the kingdom of God in regions outside of Galilee (see Mark 7:24, 31; 8:27).

After rising from the dead, Jesus instructed the female disciples to tell the other disciples to go to Galilee—for they would see Him there (see Matthew 28:10). Two of the most monumental appearances of Christ occurred in Galilee. First, Jesus appeared to several of His disciples at the Sea of Galilee. It was then that He restored Peter and said, "Follow me" (see John 21:1–23). Also in Galilee, Christ commissioned the apostles to "make disciples of all the nations, baptizing them in the name of the Father and the Son and the Holy Spirit" (see Matthew 28:16–20).

The Garden of Gethsemane

After the Last Supper, Jesus Christ and His disciples went to a place called the Garden of Gethsemane, located on the slopes of the Mount of Olives (see Luke 22:39). Gethsemane was probably in an olive grove. Just before His death, Jesus took His disciples to Gethsemane to pray in preparation for His crucifixion. Peter, James, and John fell asleep instead of praying, even despite Jesus' passionate prayer for the Father's will to be done (see Luke 22:39–46).

When Jesus finished His prayer and woke the disciples, Judas Iscariot appeared with a mob to arrest Christ. Judas then kissed Christ as a prearranged signal so they would know whom to arrest (see Matthew 26:47–49). During the arrest, Peter cut off the ear of Malchus, the high priest's servant. But Jesus healed Malchus' ear and reminded Peter that He must be arrested and crucified in order to fulfill the Scriptures (see Matthew 26:51–54; John 18:10–11).

The Garden Tomb

The Garden Tomb was the burial site of Jesus Christ. Unlike tombs today, this tomb was carved out of a rock with the entrance covered by a large stone. Luke, in his Gospel, tells us that it was a new tomb where no one had ever been laid (see Luke 23:53).

Golgatha (Calvary)

Jesus Christ was crucified between two criminals at Golgatha. It was located on an elevated site somewhere near Jerusalem and close to the Garden Tomb, where Jesus was buried (see Matthew 27:33; Mark 15:22; John 19:17, 41). The Bible also refers to Golgatha as Calvary in his Gospel, which means "skull" or "cranium."

Herod Antipas

Son of Herod the Great, Herod Antipas (or Herod the tetrarch) ruled over the regions of Galilee and Perea from 4 B.C. to A.D. 39. Antipas was famous for beheading John the Baptist, something the people of his jurisdiction resented (see Matthew 14:3–12; Mark 6:17–29; Luke 3:19–20).

Herod Antipas' role in the story of Christ is small but significant. For various political reasons and in an attempt to escape having to try Jesus Christ, Pontius Pilate (Roman Governor of Judea) handed over Jesus to Antipas to be tried, since Jesus was from Antipas' territory of Galilee. Antipas questioned and mocked Jesus, dressing Him in a royal robe, but made no judgment. Antipas then sent Jesus back to Pilate for trial in fear that Pilate would report him to the emperor.

James (Son of Alphaeus)

Sometimes identified as "James the younger" (see Mark 15:40; Matthew 27:56), James was among the apostles who were present at the Mount of Olives to witness the ascension of Jesus Christ (see Acts 1:9–13).

James (Son of Zebedee)

James was the brother of John and was one of the first apostles to be called by Jesus Christ. James, his brother, and Peter all were part of Jesus' inner circle. He was likely among the disciples who met the risen Christ at the Sea of Galilee (see John 21:1–12). After following Christ to the Mount of Olives, James was among the privileged who witnessed Christ ascend into heaven (see Luke 24:50–52;

Acts 1:9–13). James was the first of the apostles to be martyred because of their faith (see Acts 12:2).

Jerusalem

The famous capital of Palestine during Old Testament times, Jerusalem had been conquered by the Romans and was reduced to a city-state by the time of the New Testament.

Jerusalem was the location of Jesus Christ's arrest, conviction, and crucifixion. After the Resurrection, Jerusalem became the setting of the following important events:

- Jesus' appearance to the two disciples on the Emmaus road (see Mark 16:12)
- Jesus' appearance to the Eleven (see John 20:19–25)
- The ascension of Christ (see Luke 24:50; Acts 1:9–12)
- The prayer meeting in the upper room (see Acts 1:13)
- Pentecost (see Acts 2:1)

Jesus Christ

Jesus of Nazareth was God's promised Christ (anointed one), who was born to die for the sins of the world (see John 3:16). The Gospel of John tells us Jesus existed in the beginning of time and was with God and was God (see John 1:1). Christ was therefore fully God and fully man. He was born of a virgin in Bethlehem and raised in Nazareth. He grew up like a normal person, raised by His parents Mary and Joseph. But unlike the rest of us, Jesus lived a sinless life. He did, however, experience the temptations that everyday people encounter in everyday life (see Matthew 4).

Jesus began His public ministry at the age of thirty. His ministry consisted of the calling of the apostles, healing the sick, raising the dead, refuting many of the religious leaders, and preaching the kingdom of God and the repentance of sins. He ministered largely in Judea, Samaria, Galilee, and was arrested and condemned in Jerusalem, where He died on the cross for the sins of humankind. The Crucifixion was not the end of Jesus Christ. Three days later,

Christ fulfilled the Scriptures when God raised Him from the dead. This was not a mere resuscitation like Lazarus' rising from the dead. Lazarus would one day die again, but Christ would never again face death. The Resurrection assures humankind that Christ's death was effective. Sin and death did not defeat Christ, but rather, Christ defeated sin and death. His resurrection means a "new and living way which He consecrated for us" (Hebrews 10:20). Believers through Christ are now reconciled to God. The Crucifixion and Resurrection assure believers in Christ that they have the hope of life everlasting.

After the Resurrection, Jesus appeared to His disciples and to five hundred other believers during a period of forty days. In this time, Jesus provided hope to His followers and commissioned them to be His witnesses to the world until He returns again. Forty days after He was raised from the dead, Christ took His disciples to the Mount of Olives where He ascended into heaven. Later, on the day of Pentecost, the Holy Spirit came upon the believers and empowered them to live for God in spirit and in truth.

Joanna

Joanna, the wife of Chuza (see Luke 8:3), was a follower of Jesus Christ who helped provide for Jesus and His disciples while they toured Galilee (see Luke 8:2). Joanna was one of the women who helped prepare spices and ointment for Christ's body. She also was among the women who discovered the empty tomb and told the story to the disciples, who did not believe what they had to say (see Luke 24:1–11).

John (the Son of Zebedee)

The brother of James and one of the three members of Jesus' inner circle of disciples, the Apostle John was known as "the disciple whom Jesus Christ loved" (see John 19:26). John was the only disciple loyal enough to witness Christ's crucifixion. It was at the foot of the cross that Jesus commissioned John to watch over His mother, Mary. After hearing about the empty tomb, John outran Simon Peter and was the first apostle to see that the tomb was empty (see John 19:25–27). The Apostle Paul later told the church in Galatia that John was one of the three pillars of the church (see Galatians 2:9).

Joseph of Arimathea
Joseph of Arimathea was a member of the Sanhedrin and a secret follower of Christ who paid respect and honor to Christ by providing Him with a proper burial. Joseph's provision of a proper burial for Christ is marked by the clean linen and embalming oil in which he and Nicodemus wrapped Jesus Christ's body and the new tomb in which he laid Jesus (see Matthew 27:59–60; Luke 23:53; John 19:38–42). Joseph, therefore, helped to provide Christ with a burial fit for a king.

Joseph Called Barsabbas
A follower of Christ, Joseph, called Barsabbas and surnamed Justus, was nominated along with Matthias to replace Judas Iscariot as the twelfth apostle (see Acts 1:23). However, the Lord chose Matthias to take Judas' place as the twelfth apostle (see Acts 1:26).

Joseph Caiaphas the High Priest
Joseph Caiaphas was the high priest from A.D. 18–36/37. He was son-in-law to Annas, the former high priest. He was an expert politician who was convinced that Jesus Christ's death would lead to political peace. After being interrogated by Annas, Jesus was delivered to Caiaphas for a treacherous nighttime trial, where Caiaphas and the leaders attempted to find false testimony against Jesus (see Matthew 26:59–68; Mark 14:55–65; Luke 22:63–65; John 18:24). When no adequate false testimony was found, Caiaphas asked Jesus if He was the Messiah, the Son of the blessed God (see Mark 14:61). Jesus answered, "I am," and Caiaphas falsely accused Him of blasphemy and stated Jesus deserved the death sentence (see Matthew 26:65–66; Mark 14:60–63). Caiaphas was yet another person involved in the unjust trial and conviction of Christ.

Judas Iscariot

Judas Iscariot is infamous for being the disciple who betrayed Christ. He initiated his betrayal in Bethany when he met with the leading priests to betray Christ for the price of 30 pieces of silver (see Matthew 26:6–13; Mark 14:3–10). Judas finalized the deal by identifying Jesus Christ to His arresters in the Garden of Gethsemane, where Jesus was arrested (see Matthew 26:47; Mark 14:43; Luke 22:47; John 18:3–5).

The Gospels do reveal that Judas regretted his actions and went to the leading priests and tried to right his wrong by returning the money and confessing to them that he had "betrayed an innocent man" (Matthew 27:4). The priests, however, rejected the money and would have nothing to do with him. More than likely sickened by the outcome of his actions, Judas threw the money on the floor of the Temple and went out and hung himself (see Matthew 27:5).

The Apostle Peter mentioned Judas when he addressed 120 believers in Jerusalem. It was there that Peter and the rest of the apostles nominated two candidates, Joseph and Matthias, to replace Judas as the twelfth apostle. Peter did not speak highly of Judas (see Acts 1:25).

Judas, Son of James (Thaddaeus)

The Gospels of Matthew and Mark both name this apostle as Thaddaeus (see Mark 3:18; Matthew 10:3), while the Gospels of Luke and John call him Judas the son of James (see Luke 6:16; Acts 1:13; John 14:22). Judas, more than likely, was his given name while Thaddaeus was a place name or nickname. During the events of the Resurrection, Judas was only mentioned as being present at the Mount of Olives for Christ's ascension into heaven (see Acts 1:9–13).

Malchus, the High Priest's Servant

At the arrest of Jesus Christ, Peter, in an attempt to free Jesus, cut off Malchus' ear with a sword. Jesus then commanded Peter to put away his sword, reminding Peter that He was supposed to die for humankind (see John 18:11; Matthew 26:51–56). Jesus then touched Malchus' ear and healed it (see Luke 22:51).

Mary Magdalene

A follower of Jesus Christ from the time He visited cities and villages to announce the Good News of the kingdom of God (see Luke 8:2), Mary was among the last at the cross and the first at Jesus Christ's tomb on Easter morning. Her status among the women is evident in that she is always listed first when Scripture names groups of the female followers of Christ. All four Gospels record Mary, along with the other female disciples, as the first to discover that Christ's tomb was empty (see Matthew 28:1–10; Mark 16:1–8; Luke 24:1–12). Mary had the honor of being the first person to whom the resurrected Christ appeared. The Gospel of John records that Jesus commissioned her to find the disciples and proclaim the message: "I have seen the Lord!" (see John 20:14–18). Mary Magdalene proved to be a devoted follower of Christ, who ministered to Him from beginning to end.

Mary, the Mother of James

Like the other female disciples, Mary was a woman of deep commitment and faith. Comparing the parallel texts of Mark 15:47; 16:1; and Luke 24:10, it is likely that Mary was the "other Mary" of Matthew 27:61 and 28:1. She also was part of the first group of women to appear at the empty tomb (see Matthew 28:1; Mark 16:1; Luke 24:1). With the other female followers, she had the privilege of announcing the news of the Resurrection to the disciples (see Luke 24:10).

Mary, the Mother of Jesus

The early portions of the Gospels record that Mary was a young Jewish virgin engaged to a man named Joseph. God had sent the angel Gabriel to announce to her that she was "blessed among women" (Luke 1:42), because He had privileged her with giving birth to the Savior of the world. At the Crucifixion, it was apparent that Jesus Christ's death would alter the mere mother/son relationship between Jesus and Mary. At the cross, Mary had a new relationship with Christ: the relationship of her as follower and Christ as Lord. After Christ's ascension into heaven, Mary was present in the upper room, praying continually with the other disciples (see Acts 1:14).

Matthew (the Tax Collector)

Matthew, also called Levi, was a tax collector whom Jesus Christ called to be His disciple. Matthew responded by leaving everything and following Christ (see Mark 2:14; Luke 5:27–29). Scripture mentions Matthew in all four listings of the apostles (see Matthew 10:3; Mark 3:18; Luke 6:15; Acts 1:13). He also witnessed Christ's ascension and met for prayer with the other believers in the upper room (see Acts 1:12–14). Matthew also was the author of the Gospel of the same name.

Matthias

After Christ ascended into heaven, Peter addressed the need for a twelfth apostle to replace Judas Iscariot. Peter established a criteria for the election of the twelfth apostle, namely that the candidate would have to have been present from the time John the Baptist baptized Christ to the day He ascended into heaven (see Acts 1:21–22). The apostles therefore nominated two men: Matthias and Joseph called Barsabbas. Using the Old Testament manner for discovering the choice of God (see Proverbs 16:33), the apostles cast lots and Matthias was chosen. No other scriptural information exists concerning Matthias, but church tradition states that he preached in Judea and that he was later stoned to death.

Mount of Olives

In His final week, Jesus Christ taught on the Mount of Olives and spent His nights there as well (see Mark 13; Luke 21:37). The Mount of Olives is a rounded hill reaching 2,676 feet high and overlooked the Temple. After the Last Supper, Jesus brought His disciples to the Mount of Olives, where they prayed nearby in the Garden of Gethsemane. Immediately after praying, Jesus was arrested at Gethsemane. The Mount of Olives was also the location where the disciples witnessed Christ's ascension (see Mark 14:32; Acts 1:12).

Nathanael

See Bartholomew

Nicodemus

Nicodemus was a Pharisee and a member of the Sanhedrin. Nicodemus met with Jesus Christ at night and discussed with Him the need to be born again (see John 3). He later openly defended Christ before the Sanhedrin. Nicodemus helped Joseph of Arimathea provide Jesus with a proper burial. Nicodemus was most likely among the many who believed in Christ, but did not confess their belief in fear that they would be excommunicated (see John 12:42). Christian tradition states that Nicodemus was indeed a believer.

Peter (Simon)

Peter was the famous follower of Jesus Christ whom the Bible depicts as the leader of the 12 apostles. Peter's birth name was Simon, but Jesus renamed him *Peter*, which means "rock."

At the Last Supper, he boldly protested any possibility that he could deny Jesus, insisting that he would die before ever denying Him (see Matthew 26:35). All four Gospel writers depict Peter's threefold denial of Christ just before His crucifixion (see Matthew 26:69–75; Mark 14:66–72; Luke 22:55–62; John 18: 25–27). The Gospel of John records a unique meeting between the risen Christ and Peter, where Jesus restored Peter, telling him "feed my sheep" and "follow me" (see John 21:17, 19).

Peter and the Apostle John were the first disciples to see the empty tomb on Easter Sunday (see Luke 24:12; 20:3–10). Peter witnessed Christ's ascension into heaven and prayed along with the other disciples in the upper room (see Acts 1:12–14). Shortly thereafter, he addressed the disciples and led them in the nomination and selection of Matthias as the twelfth apostle. Peter later became one of the central leaders of the early church. He eventually died a martyr's death under Nero's persecution of the Christians.

Philip

Not to be mistaken with Philip the evangelist (see Acts 21:8), Philip was one of the first apostles to follow Christ (see John 1:35–51).

Like the other apostles, Philip witnessed the Ascension and was present for the choosing of Matthias as the twelfth apostle.

Pontius Pilate

Pontius Pilate was Roman governor (or prefect) of Judea from A.D 26–36/37 and was a key political figure. Early in the morning, on the day of Christ's death, the Jewish leaders brought Christ before Pontius Pilate, accusing Jesus Christ of claiming to be king. Pilate desired to release Jesus because of His innocence, knowing the chief priests handed over Jesus due to envy. The crowds, however, were relentless at Christ's trial, demanding for Him to be crucified. Pilate then gave in and took water and washed his hands clean, saying "I am innocent of the blood of this just Person." (Matthew 27:24). The crowds yelled in agreement and Pilate had Jesus scourged and handed over for crucifixion.

The day after the Crucifixion, the leading priests and Pharisees came to Pilate and reminded him that Christ had predicted He would rise from the dead in three days. To prevent any resurrection stories, the religious leaders asked Pilate to seal the tomb and have it protected by Roman guards. This way no one could steal the body of Christ. Pilate appeased the religious leaders and granted their wishes (see Matthew 27:62–66).

But on the third day, an angel rolled away the stone of the tomb, revealing that Christ had indeed risen from the dead (see Matthew 28:1–7). Shortly thereafter, Pilate was recalled from his place of office. The tradition of the church states that he later committed suicide.

Pontius Pilate's Wife

Claudia Procula, Pontius Pilate's wife, appears on the scene during the trial of Christ. Just as Pilate was attempting to free Christ, she sent him a message concerning Jesus Christ. The message read: "Have nothing to do with that just Man, for I have suffered many things today in a dream because of Him" (Matthew 27:19). Despite her wise counsel, Pilate gave into the wishes of the crowds and had Jesus scourged and crucified.

Potter's Field

See "Field of Blood (*Akeldama*)"

The Praetorium

The Praetorium was the residence of Pontius Pilate, governor of Judea. It was here that Pilate questioned Jesus Christ before His crucifixion (see John 18:28). The word *praetorium* can also loosely refer to another part of the residence, such as where the Roman soldiers mocked Jesus after He appeared before Pilate (see Matthew 27:27–31; Mark 15:16–20).

The Residence and Courtyard of Caiaphas and Annas

Joseph Caiaphas the high priest and Annas the former high priest lived in different wings of the same residence. In the courtyard of this residence is where Peter's denial takes place while Annas interrogated Jesus inside the residence. Annas then sent Jesus to Caiaphas for trial, which occurred in another area of the home (see Matthew 26:57–58; Mark 14:53–54; Luke 22:54–55; John 18:19–24).

The Roman Centurion

The Roman centurion at the cross was so impressed by Jesus Christ's death that he made the statement, "Truly, this man was the Son of God!" (Mark 15:39). The centurion's words may have been a profession of faith in Christ or he may have simply meant that Jesus was a righteous and innocent man, as Luke states it (see Luke 23:47). Either way, the Roman centurion's statement is further evidence that the political and religious leaders of the day were guilty of crucifying the innocent Christ, who was indeed the Son of God.

Salome

Salome was a faithful follower of Jesus Christ and helped care for Him while He was in Galilee. Salome is seen at the foot of the cross with Mary Magdalene and Mary the mother of James (see Mark 15:41). After Christ's death, these women brought spices to anoint Christ's body for burial (see Mark 16:1). Salome is an example of a loving and faithful follower of Christ who helped care for Him even when most deserted Him.

Sanhedrin

The Sanhedrin was the supreme Jewish council in Jerusalem during the times of the New Testament. It presided over the religious, political, and legal issues of all Jews. The Sanhedrin's membership consisted of seventy-one Jewish leaders. The head of the Sanhedrin was the high priest (see Matthew 26:57). After Herod the Great's reign, religious reasons ceased to be the primary means for choosing the high priest. More often than not, he was appointed for political reasons. Under the high priest was the captain of the Temple (see Luke 22:4, 52). The rest of the members were select Levites and priests. The Gospels seem to point to the chief priests, former high priests who belonged to the Sadducees, as the central members of the Sanhedrin (see Acts 4:1; 5:17). The Bible provides evidence that Pharisees were members of the Sanhedrin as well (see John 3:1). The Sanhedrin was partly responsible for the planning and carrying out of Christ's trial (see Matthew 26:59; Mark 14:55; 15:1; John 11:47–53).

Satan

Satan was an exalted angelic being who became proud and attempted to dethrone God (see Isaiah 14:12–14; Ezekiel 28:11–19). God, who is in control of all things, removed Satan from his position of honor. Satan then convinced one-third of the angels to follow him in his mission to usurp the plans of God.

Although Satan played a part in tempting both Judas Iscariot and Peter (see Luke 22:3; Luke 22:31), the crucifixion was not the result of Satan's doing. It was Christ's intended purpose to die on the cross for the sins of the world (see John 3:16).

The Sea of Galilee

Famous for being the setting of many New Testament events (see Matthew 8:23–27; Mark 5:1–13, 35–41; Luke 8:22–24; John 6:15–21), the Sea of Galilee is located in the Jordan Valley; its surface sits at 696 feet below sea level. This body of water is approximately thirteen miles long and eight miles wide.

After Jesus rose from the dead, He appeared to the disciples as they were fishing at the Sea of Galilee. Jesus yelled out to them, asking if they caught any fish. Unable to see who Jesus was, the disciples told Him no and were directed by Christ to cast their net on the right side of the boat. The disciples obeyed and caught so many fish that they were not able to draw in the net. Suddenly, the disciples realized that the man standing on the shore was Jesus, their Lord (see John 21:5–13).

Simon of Cyrene
Simon was from Cyrene, a district of North Africa. On the road to Golgotha, the Romans forced Simon to carry Jesus Christ's cross (see Matthew 27:32; Mark 15:21; Luke 23:26). Simon was the father of Alexander and Rufus. In his letter to the Romans, the Apostle Paul said Rufus was chosen of the Lord; he also stated that Rufus' mother had been a mother to him as well (see Romans 16:13). From Paul's words, we can presume Simon may have later become a Christian.

Simon (the Zealot)
One of the twelve apostles of Jesus Christ, Simon was a zealot. Zealots were members of a revolutionary political group that believed political submission to Rome denied God as Lord. The Gospels of Matthew and Mark refer to Simon as the "Cananaean," which is from the Aramaic word for *zealot* (see Matthew 10:4; Mark 3:18). The dynamics of the apostles are apparent with the call of Simon the zealot and Matthew the tax collector. Tax collectors and zealots held political beliefs that were on opposing ends of the political spectrum. After the Resurrection, Simon, like the rest of the eleven apostles, was present for Christ's ascension into heaven, for the corporate prayer in the upper room, and for the election of Matthias as Judas' replacement (see Acts 1:12–26).

The Temple
See "The First Century Temple"

Thaddaeus
See Judas (Son of James)

Thomas

Improperly known as "doubting Thomas," the Gospel of John depicts this apostle as a strong, faithful, and courageous man of character. Thomas' boldness is evident in his words to the apostles, "Let us also go, that we may die with Him" (John 11:16). But he is most famous for missing the first appearance of the risen Christ (see John 20:19–24), and then refusing to believe that Jesus was alive until He saw Jesus Christ and the wounds on His body. Eight days later, Jesus granted Thomas' request and appeared before him and the other disciples. Jesus said to Thomas, "Put your finger here and see my hands. Put your hand into the wound in my side. Don't be faithless any longer. Believe!" Thomas replied with one of the New Testament's most profound and monumental confessions of Christ's deity: "My Lord and my God!" (John 20:28). Afterward, Thomas was present with the other apostles for the Ascension, for the corporate prayer in the upper room, and for the election of Matthias as the replacement of Judas Iscariot as the twelfth apostle (see Acts 1:12–26).

The Upper Room

In biblical times, some homes had second-story rooms, which resembled towers. These rooms were often referred to as "upper rooms." Jesus Christ and His disciples ate the Passover supper in an upper room. After the Ascension, Luke wrote that the apostles returned to Jerusalem and went to the upper room of the house where they were staying (see Acts 1:12–13). It was most likely there that the apostles prayed continually with the other followers of Christ (see Acts 1:14).

THE CHRONOLOGY OF THE CROSS

To help you understand what Jesus Christ went through during the time before His death, here is a chronology of events.

KEY EVENTS	TIME OF DAY
Christ and the Disciples Eat the Last Supper	Thursday Evening
Christ Prays in the Garden of Gethsemane and Is Then Betrayed and Arrested	Thursday Evening
Annas the Former High Priest Interrogates Christ	Thursday Night before Midnight
Joseph Caiaphas, the High Priest, Begins Formal Trial of Christ	Friday Morning Sometime after Midnight
The High Priest's Questioning of Christ	Early Friday Morning
Peter's Denial of Christ	Friday Morning around 3 A.M. (the time of the cockcrow in Jerusalem
The Mocking of Christ	Early Friday Morning
The Jewish Trial Ends with the Sanhedrin's Decision against Christ	Friday Morning As Day Was Dawning
Christ Led to Pontius Pilate and Accused of Sedition	Friday Morning
Judas Iscariot Hangs Himself	Friday Morning
Christ's Initial Hearing before Pontius Pilate	Friday Morning
Pilate Hands Christ over to Herod Antipas; Herod Mocks Christ	Friday Morning
Pontius Pilate and Herod Antipas Are Reconciled	Friday Morning
Pontius Pilate Resumes the Trial of Christ; Christ is Scourged and Mocked	Friday Morning
Christ on the Road to the Cross	Friday Sometime before 9:00 A.M.
Christ Is Crucified	Friday from 9:00 A.M. to 3:00 P.M.
Christ Is Buried	Friday Evening As Evening Approached
Christ in the Tomb	Saturday
Christ Rises from the Dead	Sunday Morning As the New Day Was Dawning

BOOK OF MATTHEW	BOOK OF MARK	BOOK OF LUKE	BOOK OF JOHN
26:20–29	14:17–25	22:14–38	13:2–4
26:36-56	14:26–52	22:39–53	18:1–12
			18:13
26:57	14:53	22:54	18:24
26:59–68	14:55–65		18:19–24
26:69–75	14:66–72	22:55–62	18:15–18, 25–27
		22:63–65	
27:1	15:1a	22:66–71	
27:2	15:1b	23:1	18:28
27:3–10			
27:11–14	15:2–5	23:2–6	18:29–40
		23:7–11	
		23:12	
27:17–31	15:8–20	23:13–25	19:1–16
27:32–34	15:21–23	23:26–32	19:17
27:35	15:25	23:33	19:18
27:57–61	15:42–47	23:50–55	19:38–42
27:62–65	16:1	23:56	
28:1–15	16:1–8	24:1–35	20:1–18

"**Father, into**
YOUR HANDS
I Commit
MY SPIRIT."
LUKE
23:46

CHAPTER 5

SEVEN STATEMENTS FROM THE CROSS

Examining the significance of the words
Jesus uttered before His death

The seven statements Jesus Christ made from the cross give us a glimpse into the eternal and show us that our salvation was paid in full, once and for all, at the cross. The final words of the dying capture our attention, often reveal the speaker's character, and can even impart wisdom for our own lives. The final words of Jesus do that and much more.

Statement One
"Father, forgive them for they do not know what they do."

The fact that Jesus' first words from the cross consisted of a prayer does not surprise us. Jesus always had been a man of prayer.

But we might have expected Jesus to pray, "Father, help Me!" Or, even His later statement being His first: "My God, My God, why have you forsaken Me?" But knowing Jesus, it was only fitting that He should say what He said in the very order He said it.

He did not pray in that dark hour for His loved ones first, or for His friends. He prayed for His enemies! He modeled exactly what He taught.

We also see from this example of Jesus that no one is beyond the reach of prayer. No matter how hopeless it may look, keep praying for that person! It was as if Jesus was saying, "Father, forgive them, for they need forgiveness so desperately…Forgive them, for they have committed a sin that is wicked beyond all comprehension… Forgive them, for they have committed a sin that is black beyond all their realization."

Maybe you're praying for someone right now to see his or her need for God. You've brought that friend to church, but there's no apparent interest in spiritual things. Keep praying!

Statement Two
"Today you will be with Me in Paradise."

His second statement was an answer to prayer. Next to Jesus were two criminals being crucified. Something significant happened to change the heart of one of these criminals, bringing him to his spiritual senses. Jesus' second statement was an answer to that prayer for forgiveness. Jesus spoke to that criminal as though he were the only person in the world.

What joy must have filled this man's heart when he heard these words! We cannot help but notice this man's immediate faith: "Lord, remember me when You come into Your kingdom."

He did not say, "Remember me if you come into Your kingdom," but rather, "Remember me *when* you come into Your kingdom" (Luke 23:42, emphasis added).

It would seem at this moment that this thief, who only had come alive spiritually just moments before, had more spiritual insight than many of Jesus' closest followers!

Also, I love the way this new convert defends Jesus to the other criminal: "Do you not even fear God, seeing you are under the same condemnation? And we indeed justly, for we receive the due reward of our deeds; but this Man has done nothing wrong" (Luke 23:40–41).

Amazingly, both men heard these words of Jesus. Both saw His flawless and incredible example. Both were dying, and both needed forgiveness. The unrepentant thief died as he had lived, hardened and indifferent. The other repented, believed, and as a result, joined Jesus in Paradise.

The mystery of the gospel! Hearing the same message, one person will listen with indifference while another will have his or her eyes opened to his or her needs and will believe.

Statement Three
"Woman, behold your son."

The Lord's third statement from the cross was a response to what He saw. At the foot of the cross was His mother Mary, along with some other women and John the apostle. Looking down at Mary and John, He said to His mother, "Woman, behold your son." Then He said to John, "Behold your mother." From that hour, John took Mary into his home. The Lord was thinking about the needs of His mother and her future on earth.

Statement Four
"My God, My God, why have You forsaken Me?"

At noon, darkness suddenly fell on the earth. Piercing through that darkness was Christ' voice as He cried out, *"Eli, Eli, lama sabachthani?"* (Matthew 27:46; see also Mark 15:34).

It was at this moment that I believe Jesus bore all the sins of the world. Every wicked thing ever done by every person was poured on Jesus at that very moment. In my opinion, it was God's most painful moment.

You would think, as a moment like this was unfolding, that the people would stand in complete silence, especially when darkness fell on the earth. But as we read the crucifixion account, we realize that the mockery continued until the very end. Even as He was bearing the sins of the world and crying out, *"Eli, Eli, lama sabachthani?"* they had no interest at all. People were laughing, mocking, gambling, and acting as though nothing of any importance was taking place. In reality, the most significant event in human history was unfolding.

Statement Five
"I thirst!"

We find the next words that Jesus gave from the cross in John 19:28–29:

> After this, Jesus, knowing that all things were now accomplished, that the Scripture might be fulfilled, said, "I thirst!" Now a vessel full of sour wine was sitting there; and they filled a sponge with sour wine, put it on hyssop, and put it to His mouth.

"I thirst!" was the first from the lips of our Lord of a personal nature. Understand that this was not merely a casual thirst. This was a thirst produced by a tremendous loss of blood. This was a thirst produced by a man who had literally borne the sins of the world. This was a thirst like no man has ever known before. Imagine the Creator of the universe, God Almighty, saying, "I thirst!" The very One who created water was crying out for just a few drops to quench His insatiable thirst.

"I thirst," was a statement Jesus said to the woman at the well when He asked for a drink of water. Again, as He was hanging on the cross, He said, "I thirst." Here is what it comes down to: because Jesus thirsted, we don't have to. Because He died on the cross, we don't have to be thirsty. He has made possible a way for us to know God. No longer do we have to go thirsting after the empty things this world offers. We can satisfy our thirst in a relationship with Him.

You may recall that prior to this moment, Jesus was offered sour wine mingled with gall—basically, a painkiller. You might also remember that the Lord refused it (see Matthew 27:34). He was going to bear the Crucifixion and all of its pain. He would take upon Himself the sin of the world and all of its horror, and He wanted to have full sense of His mental faculties.

Statement Six
"It is finished!"

Now, having borne the sins of the world, Jesus cries out "It is finished!" (John 19:30). This battle cry of the cross was the greatest and most far-reaching battle cry ever heard in history. Those who stood close—Mary, John, the Roman soldiers, and others—were not the only ones who heard these three words. I believe these words echoed throughout heaven. I am sure they were heard as a cry of victory among the angels who would have, at any moment, come and gladly delivered the Lord from this situation. "It is finished."

I also think these words reverberated throughout the hallways of hell as Satan realized his plan had backfired. In his blind rage and jealousy, Satan had filled the heart of Judas Iscariot to betray the Lord, but he actually helped bring about the completion of God's plan. He unwittingly played into the plan and purpose of the Father, who determined long ago that God would come to this earth as a man and die on a cross. It is spoken of extensively in the Old Testament. Suddenly, perhaps at this moment, it dawned on the devil that he just helped fulfill prophetic scriptures. He helped bring about the purposes of God. What was meant to destroy Jesus would now ultimately destroy the devil.

What does this phrase, "It is finished," mean? It could be translated a number of ways: *It is made an end of. It is paid. It is performed. It is accomplished.* Each one of those phrases gives a different facet to the meaning of "It is finished."

What was made an end of?
Our slavery to sin and the guilt that accompanies it.
What was paid? The price of our redemption.
What was performed? The righteous requirements of the law.
What was accomplished? All that the Father had given Jesus to do.

The storm had finally passed. The devil had done his worst and the Lord had bruised Him. Now the darkness has ended, and it is finished. Understand this was a victory cry from Calvary. This was a glorious moment because the work was now completed.

What was finished? Finished were the horrendous sufferings of Christ. Never again would He experience pain or be in the hands of Satan. Never again would He bear the sins of the world. Never again would He, even for a moment, be forsaken of God. Finished were the demands of the Mosaic Law, those standards laid out in the Scripture that we were unable to keep.

Satan's stronghold on humanity was finished. Because of what Jesus did on the cross, we no longer have to be under the power of Satan.

This does not mean we never will be tempted. It does not mean we are not vulnerable to the enticements of the devil. But it does mean that Satan has no rights over our lives. We were under his control, but Jesus suffered for our redemption. Jesus came and died for our freedom. This is what happened for us at Calvary. The humility, the sorrow, the suffering, the separation, the love— that is the passion of Jesus Christ.

Therefore, we no longer have to be under the power of any sin if we don't want to be. We don't have to be under the power of immorality. We don't have to be under the power of addiction to drugs or alcohol. We don't have to be under the power of any vice or any lifestyle. We have been freed by the work that Jesus performed on the cross. He has opened the door to our prison cells, but each of us must get up and walk out.

Some of us don't really want to be freed from the vice that may have a strangle-hold on our lives. Some of us don't want to change. Some of us don't want to get out of the darkness we are in. I am telling you on the authority of Scripture that if you want out, the door is open. Jesus Christ has paid the price. He will give you the power and resources to be victorious over the power of sin. Your life may not be sinless, but you can sin *less*. Your life can be transformed because of what was finished on the cross.

Finished was our salvation. All our sins were transferred to Jesus when He hung on the cross, and righteousness was transferred to our account. As Isaiah 53:6 says, "The Lord has laid on Him the iniquity of us all." It is finished. There is nothing that you or I can add to the work that Jesus did for us.

It is all paid—no more debts left. Jesus has done this for you and for me. "It is finished."

Statement Seven
"Into Your hands I commit My spirit."

Jesus then gives His seventh and final statement from the cross. He says to the Father, "Into Your hands I commit My spirit" (Luke 23:46). The Lord often said: "No one takes it [my life] from Me, but I lay it down of Myself. I have power to lay it down, and I have power to take it again" (John 10:18). The Roman soldiers who came to break Jesus' legs were amazed that He already had died. This practice was intended to prevent the one on the cross from pulling up for a breath. As a result, the prisoner would immediately die of suffocation. When they came to Jesus, it was not necessary to break His bones, which fulfilled the Scripture that says not one of His bones would be broken (see Exodus 12:46; Numbers 9:12; Psalm 34:20; John 19:36).

Christ made His love for the world passionately evident in these last statements from the cross, and the presentation of these statements in all their pain, victory, and meaning is powerful to behold:

"Father, forgive them for they do not know what they do."
Do you realize that you are in need of the Father's forgiveness?

"Today you will be with Me in Paradise."
Have you realized and confessed Jesus as your personal Savior?

"Woman behold your son."
Jesus is concerned and provides for all of us.

"My God, My God, why have You forsaken Me?"
Jesus was forsaken so we don't have to be.

"I thirst!"
This personal statement reminds us that Jesus is not only God, but He was also man. Jesus identifies with our needs.

"It is finished."
Our sin is paid for and sin's control over our lives is broken!

"Into Your hands I commit My spirit."
You can trust your life into God's hands.

―❧―

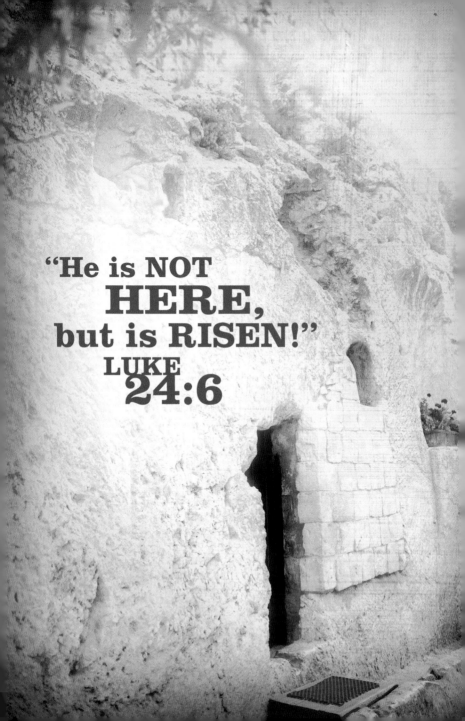

CHAPTER 6

WHAT HAPPENED EASTER MORNING

"Very early on Sunday morning, everything changed.
Hope had arisen!"

A while back, the cover of *Time* featured a painting of Jesus Christ that introduced a series of articles about His impact not only on our time, but also on all of humanity for all time. Reynolds Price, the writer of one of the articles, made this statement: "A serious argument can be made that no one else's life has proved remotely as powerful and enduring as that of Jesus."

That is true. There has never been, nor will there ever be, anyone like Jesus. He stands out from all others. Because Jesus died and rose again, His life proved to be powerful and enduring. His death and resurrection transformed the lives of those who believed on Easter morning, and continually transforms the lives of those who believe today.

Lost in Translation

I've heard that when Coca-Cola was introduced in China, it was first rendered as "Ke-kou-ke-la." Unfortunately, it wasn't until after thousands of signs had been printed the company discovered the phrase means, "Bite the wax tadpole," or "Female horse stuffed with wax," depending on the dialect. And in Taiwan, the translation of the Pepsi slogan, "Come alive with the Pepsi Generation," was translated, "Pepsi will bring your ancestors back from the dead." Sometimes things get lost in the translation!

That is what happened to the followers of Christ after His crucifixion. Jesus had spoken to the disciples about His impending death and resurrection constantly and in great detail. Nevertheless, the disciples incorrectly thought Christ was going to overthrow the Roman government and establish an earthly kingdom. Therefore, the dreams of the disciples were destroyed when they saw Jesus crucified on a Roman cross. The One called the King of kings was taken and crowned with thorns. They saw spikes driven through His hands and feet. They hoped for a last-minute miracle. But none came. Their Lord was dead. The disciples never anticipated the Crucifixion. They misunderstood the message—it was lost in translation.

But very early Sunday morning, three days after Joseph of Arimathea laid Christ in the tomb, Jesus' message became clear. Let's read about what happened that first Easter Sunday in Luke 24:1–12:

> Now on the first day of the week, very early in the morning, they, and certain other women with them, came to the tomb bringing the spices which they had prepared. But they found the stone rolled away from the tomb. Then they went in and did not find the body of the Lord Jesus. And it happened, as they were greatly perplexed about this, that behold, two men stood by them in shining garments. Then, as they were afraid and bowed their faces to the earth, they said to them, "Why do you seek the living among the dead? He is not here, but is risen! Remember how He spoke to you when He was still in Galilee, saying, 'The Son of Man must be delivered into the hands of sinful men, and be crucified, and the third day rise again.'"
> And they remembered His words. Then they returned from the tomb and told all these things to the eleven and to all the rest. It was Mary Magdalene, Joanna, Mary the mother of James,

and the other women with them, who told these things to the apostles. And their words seemed to them like idle tales, and they did not believe them. But Peter arose and ran to the tomb; and stooping down, he saw the linen cloths lying by themselves; and he departed, marveling to himself at what had happened.

Here humanity had done its worst. Christ was put to death. The disciples left the cross, dismayed and disillusioned, the religious leaders rested in victory, and the Christ lay dead and buried in a dark garden tomb. Everything had fallen apart. But very early on Sunday morning, everything changed. Hope had arisen.

Then the female disciples of Christ came to the tomb, taking the spices they had prepared. Notice that it was the women—not the men—who were last at the cross and first at the tomb. The men were in hiding, but the women were willing to stand up for the Lord and to care for His body. Mark's Gospel tells us that Mary Magdalene, Salome, and Mary the mother of James were present among the women (see Mark 16:1). They were there to anoint His dead body. Though He was dead, their love for Him refused to dim. Their faith in Him had not failed. What they had hoped for had simply not happened. Yet those faithful followers would not abandon His dead body. They honored Him even in death.

The faithfulness of the women rewarded them with an unexpected surprise. Instead of finding the dead body of Jesus, they came face to face with holy angels of God. Then one of the angels said, "He is not here, but is risen! Remember how He spoke to you when He was still in Galilee, saying, 'The Son of Man must be delivered into the hands of sinful men, and be crucified, and the third day rise again.'" (Luke 24:6–7). Then they remembered His words. So they ran to tell the apostles. But when the apostles heard what had happened, they said that the story sounded like nonsense, so they would not believe it (see verses 10–11). These great men of faith regarded the witness of these women as mere hysteria. It's hard to believe that these were the apostles. These were the ones whom

Jesus spent an entire night praying over before He called them. Yet when they heard the message that the Lord had risen, they didn't believe it.

The Race to the Tomb

The Gospel of John does fill in a few details which reveal that two disciples investigated Mary Magdalene's testimony. To their credit, Peter and John had to see the empty tomb for themselves (see John 20:1–2). After hearing about the Resurrection, Peter and John sprinted to the tomb, but John outran Peter (see John 20:3–4). I think there is a reason why John beat Peter to the tomb, and it had little to do with who was the faster runner.

Consider this: Remember when you were a child and you got in to trouble with your mom and she uttered those ominous words, "You just wait until your father gets home!" Then when dad pulled into the driveway, I bet you did not run as quickly to meet him at the door. You knew you were going to have to come face to face with what you had done wrong. Your conscience was guilty and you feared the consequences of your actions.

In the same way, Peter's last contact with the Lord was when he denied Him. He was running to the tomb, but with mixed emotions, to say the least. Then Peter walked into the tomb. With his chest heaving from the run, he probably thought, *What's going on here? Where is the Lord? Where is His body?* Then John entered, and the Gospel tells us that "he saw and believed. For as yet they did not know the Scripture, that He must rise again from the dead" (John 20:8–9).

Don't Live in the Old Way

Now Peter and John were gone. The other women had left too. And there was Mary—all alone. She was still wondering where the body of Jesus was. She could not take it anymore. She broke under the pressure and began to weep. So the angels in the tomb asked her, "Why are you weeping?" And she replied, "Because they have taken away my Lord…and I do not know where they have laid Him" (John 20:13).

Then hope came to Mary. She heard a voice speak to her out of the darkness. It was Jesus, but she did not recognize Him at first. "Why are you weeping?" Jesus asked her. "Whom are you seeking?" She answered and said, "Sir…if you have carried him away, tell me where you have laid Him, and I will take Him away." Then Jesus said her name. "Mary!" And she realized that He was the Lord and cried out, "Teacher!" She grabbed a hold of Him, but Christ told her, "Do not cling to Me, for I have not yet ascended to My Father; but go to My brethren and say to them, 'I am ascending to My Father and your Father, and to My God and your God.'" (John 20:15–17).

Some people have tried to read some mystical meaning into this verse. They have claimed that the Lord's resurrected body was so fragile that you did not want to touch it. That is not true. In other instances people touched Him. In Matthew's Gospel, after the Resurrection, the women grabbed hold of Jesus' feet and worshipped Him. When He appeared to the disciples in the upper room and Thomas was there, Jesus told him to touch His hands and His side (see John 20:27).

I think there is a deeper meaning to why Jesus told Mary not to touch Him. It could better be translated, "Don't cling to me." Or literally, "Stop clinging to me." Jesus was essentially saying, "Mary, it is a new day. It is not going to be the way it used to be. In the old days, I would be with you physically in a given place at a given time. We would spend time together. Those days are gone. Now it is going to be better. My Holy Spirit is going to live inside of you!" Then He tells her, "I am ascending to My Father and your Father, and to My God and your God" (John 20:17). Jesus was saying, "Mary, because of what I have done at the cross and at the Resurrection, you can approach God as your Father." That was a revolutionary thought to the average Jew of the day. The Jews would refer to God by using the more formal term, *Lord*. They would rarely, if ever, use the intimate term of *Father*. Jesus was saying, "This is a new covenant that is established. Now I am going to send you My Holy Spirit. Don't cling to the old ways. Don't live in the old way.

This is a new covenant I have established." This is true for all of us as well, for the Apostle Paul wrote "For you did not receive a spirit that makes you a slave again to fear, but you received the Spirit of sonship. And by him we cry, '*Abba*, Father' " (Romans 8:15 NIV).

The Bible says that Christ has done all of that for us. He has opened for us a new and a living way. Mary was so excited about seeing the Lord and hearing His message that she could not wait to tell the others. John 20:18 says, "Mary Magdalene came and told the disciples that she had seen the Lord, and that He had spoken these things to her."

The message of Christ's resurrection transformed everything. It transformed a group of disillusioned, discouraged, and frightened women and men into bold and courageous disciples who turned their world upside down.

Lessons from Easter Morning

There are a number of things we should learn from that first Easter morning, some two thousand years ago.

First, Easter reminds us that God loves ordinary and flawed people. They don't come any more flawed than Peter, John, and Mary. Remember, Mary was a demon-possessed woman—but Jesus healed her and transformed her life (see Luke 8:2). He not only forgave her but also commissioned her to go and take this message to the world. This gives hope to all of the ordinary people out there. You, who were picked last for the team. You, who never won the contest. You, who never distinguished yourself in any significant way from the others. This message from the Resurrection reminds us that God can do extraordinary things through ordinary people.

Secondly, Easter shows us that God blesses those who seek Him with their whole heart. There is no question that Mary's persistent faith and love was richly rewarded. She was last at the cross. She was first at the tomb. She just wanted to be close to Jesus. She loved the Lord and wanted the world to know. She made time early in the morning to be with Him. If you will make time in your life and in your schedule for Jesus, He will reward you as well. The Bible says, "Great is His faithfulness; His mercies begin afresh each morning" (Lamentations 3:23 NLT). But some of us will say, "I don't have time for Bible study or prayer. I have so many things to do." If that's the case, then maybe you need to slow down and make time for what is important. God will bless you for that. Mary made time for Jesus. What a blessing she received.

The third lesson we should learn is that Easter reveals the promise that God will more than meet us halfway. Here was a woman who was weakened in her faith, but strong in her love. She came with what she had and Jesus more than met her halfway. Maybe you have a weakened faith. A tragedy has befallen you. A loved one has died. A marriage has collapsed. Your faith has suffered. Maybe in your estimation, you feel as though God has somehow let you down. God wants to renew your faith. He wants to bring you back to that place of fervency and commitment. Just as He ministered to Mary, He can minister to you as well.

Finally, Easter gives us hope for now and eternity. Mary was so excited because what appeared to have been the worst defeat imaginable, remarkably turned out to be the greatest victory of all. The fact that Jesus Christ rose from the dead means that there is hope in this life and hope after it.

In the words of the Apostle Paul, "But if the Spirit of Him who raised Jesus from the dead dwells in you, He who raised Christ from the dead will also give life to your mortal bodies through His Spirit who dwells in you." (Romans 8:11). Paul is saying that God has provided every Christian with the power to live this life He has called us to live. I admit, living the Christian life can be hard, but it is possible through the power of the Holy Spirit. The same Spirit who raised Jesus from the dead has taken residence in you. The same Holy Spirit whom Jesus breathed on the disciples is living inside of you. He will enable you to be the woman or man that God has called you to be.

But Easter also reveals the hope of life after death, because if Jesus died and rose again, we too will be raised like Him. The Apostle Paul made this point in his letter to the church in Corinth:

> But now Christ is risen from the dead, and has become the firstfruits of those who have fallen asleep. For since by man came death, by Man also came the resurrection of the dead. For as in Adam all die, even so in Christ all shall be made alive. (1 Corinthians 15:20–22)

The Bible says that you are going to fall asleep and go into the presence of God. That is the picture Scripture uses. Because Jesus died and rose again, you have life beyond the grave. Paul tells us in 1 Thessalonians 4:14, "For if we believe that Jesus died and rose again, even so God will bring with Him those who sleep in Jesus" (1 Thessalonians 4:14). Whatever stage of life you are in, this promise is precious. We, as believers, will live forever with God in heaven.

This is what happened Easter morning: God through Christ conquered sin and death, providing eternal life to anyone who believes. No other person's life—past, present, or future—has accomplished such a feat. There will never be anyone like Jesus, and because of what happened Easter morning, we will have the privilege of spending eternity with Him.

"**BLESSED** are those who have **Not Seen** and yet have **Believed.**" JOHN 20:29

CHAPTER 7

EVIDENCE FOR THE RESURRECTION

"For all practical purposes, God says,
'Believe and I will show you.'"

C hrist's resurrection from the dead is not a peripheral issue. The Resurrection is foundational to the Christian faith. In fact, it's what sets the Christian faith apart from all others. For that reason, it's easy to see why people have attempted to explain away the Resurrection. But to the dismay of skeptics throughout history, four main lines of evidence exist that help attest to the truth of the Resurrection.

The Empty Tomb

The first argument for the Resurrection is the empty tomb. That Christ's tomb was empty three days after He died is essential to Christianity—for if Christ's body was still there, then Christ did not rise from the dead. And if Christ is not alive, then our faith is in vain (see 1 Corinthians 15:14). But one look at the Gospels and it is clear that all four authors were in complete agreement that Christ's tomb was empty three days after He died. Many other witnesses verified this fact as well (see Matthew 28:5–6; Mark 16:6; Luke 24:1–3; John 20:1–2).

The oldest claim against the Resurrection was that somebody stole the body of Christ. Only two groups of people had real motives to steal the body: the followers of Christ and the enemies of Christ. And from examining history and Scripture, neither of these groups were likely candidates for robbing the tomb of Christ.

Despite the arguments throughout history, the disciples were not likely suspects for counterfeiting the Resurrection. The truth of the matter is that the followers of Christ did not even believe Christ was going to rise from the dead. Remember when the women reported the Resurrection to the disciples? The Scriptures tell us that the men thought the report of the women "seemed to them like idle tales, and they did not believe them" (Luke 24:11). Instead of waiting with great anticipation, they rejected it out of hand. It's also unlikely that the disciples—who just three days ago fled for their lives during the Crucifixion—would have suddenly mustered the courage and ingenuity to steal the body and then boldly begin preaching and teaching about a Jesus who was really dead. The facts simply do not match up. The disciples were in hiding. They were in shock and disbelief. None of Christ's followers were displaying the character it took to challenge the Roman government and steal the body of Christ. That is a dramatic change that cannot be overlooked.

The only other main suspects for the robbery of Christ's body were His enemies. The only problem with this theory is that Christ's enemies had no motive to rob His grave. The leading priests and other religious leaders put Christ to death because His teachings and His followers posed a threat to their religious system and way of life. The last thing these people wanted was another Jesus movement. That's why they had Christ crucified. And that's why the religious leaders went to great lengths to eliminate any appearance of a resurrection. The Gospel of Matthew tells us that they went to Pontius Pilate and said,

> Sir, we remember, while He was still alive, how that deceiver said, 'After three days I will rise.' Therefore command that the

tomb be made secure until the third day, lest His disciples come by night and steal Him away, and say to the people, 'He has risen from the dead.' So the last deception will be worse than the first. (Matthew 27:63–64)

Then Pilate replied, "Make it as secure as you know how." So they went and sealed the tomb and placed guards there to protect it (see Matthew 27:65–66). It sounds as though these religious leaders possessed more confidence in the resurrection of Christ than His own followers had.

The truth of the matter is that the religious leaders took extreme measures to protect Christ's body from being stolen. They wanted to prove that Christ's promise of a resurrection was a lie. The religious leaders left no room for error. They covered their bases to eliminate any chance of any stories circulating about Christ rising from the dead. Stealing the body would have accomplished everything the enemies of Christ were against. But if they had stolen the body, they undoubtedly would have produced it once that fledgling group of believers began to win people to Christ. But Jesus' enemies never produced His body, because they had no body to produce. The tomb was empty because Christ rose from the dead.

The Appearances of the Risen Lord

The eyewitness accounts of the risen Lord also attest to the truth of the Resurrection. The reality is that when Jesus was crucified, His disciples were devastated and destroyed. Their faith was to a large degree shattered. They had no hope of ever seeing Christ alive again. Yet Jesus not only appeared to the disciples on a number of occasions, He also appeared to five hundred people at one time (see 1 Corinthians 15:6).

Despite the historical documentation of these eyewitness accounts, people often claim that they are mere fabrication. But when you inspect the accounts of Christ's appearances, they look nothing like fabricated stories. Christ first appeared to Mary Magdalene—the same woman from whom Christ cast out seven demons (see Luke 8:2). To say the least, Mary was not your ideal character witness, and if you are making up a story, she would not be the first person you would have chosen.

Another notable detail is that all four Gospel writers agree that the women were the first people to receive the angelic announcement of the Resurrection. If you were fabricating a story about Christ, you probably would not have included the angel's announcement to the women. Why? Because the traditional Jewish understanding of Jesus' time was that the testimony of women was not accepted in legal situations (see Josephus, *Antiquities* 4.8.15 [219]). So if the disciples wanted to create a story that would deceive society, choosing one based on the testimony of women was less than ideal. A truly fictitious story only would have included men, for very few people during this time took into account the testimony of women. This strongly supports the validity of the testimonies concerning the appearances of Jesus Christ. The testimonies of the women, the disciples, and the five hundred eyewitnesses of the Risen Christ are all true. Jesus the Christ had truly risen.

The Martyrdom of the Apostles

If the resurrection of Christ was a mere fairytale, why would every one of the apostles go to an early grave for a lie? Experience tells us that whenever there is a conspiracy, someone always breaks. This is especially the case when the indictments start flying and the person knows they are going to serve some time. Someone will break. They always do. And when the first person does break, others will follow because everyone is trying to save his own hide.

Similarly, if the apostles had stolen the body, why wouldn't they have broken the code of silence and simply confessed the truth, when threatened with torture and death? "We stole the body," they could have said, "And I'll tell you where it is!" But this didn't happen. In fact, the apostles not only held to their stories, they even died for them. As we look over church history and tradition, every single apostle (with the exception of John) died a gruesome and painful death, because he confessed the truth of the resurrected Christ:

- Peter: In Rome, Peter was severely scourged and then crucified upside down. The position of his crucifixion was the result of his own request, for he did not feel worthy to die in the same manner as his Lord.
- Andrew (Brother of Peter): Andrew was martyred in Patrae, Achaia. It was there that he was bound to an x-shaped cross and crucified. He preached to his persecutors until he died.
- James (Son of Zebedee): The first of the apostles to be martyred, James' death is the only martyrdom of the apostles mentioned in the New Testament (see Acts 12:2). Herod Agrippa I, the grandson of Herod the Great, was responsible for beheading James.
- John (Brother of James): Tradition tells us John was put in a caldron of boiling oil, but the oil mysteriously did no harm to John. Afterward, he was banished to the island of Patmos. Though John was sentenced to death because of his faith, he was the only apostle who did not die for his belief in the risen Christ.
- Philip: This apostle was martyred in Heliopolis. He was scourged and later crucified.
- Bartholomew (Nathanael): According to the "Martyrdom of St. Bartholomew," he was put in a sack and thrown into the sea. Another source claims he was crucified upside down after being flayed alive.
- Thomas: This apostle of Christ was run through the body with a lance in India.
- Matthew (or Levi, the Tax Collector): Matthew was slain in distant Ethiopia.
- James (Son of Alphaeus): The Apostle James was stoned and then beaten to death with a club.
- Judas, Son of James (Thaddaeus): Church tradition is not clear on the martyrdom of this apostle. One account states he was crucified, while another tradition claims he was shot to death with arrows.

- Simon (the Zealot): The reports of church history tell us that Simon was crucified after preaching the gospel.

If the Resurrection was a lie, a fabrication, don't you think at least one of the apostles would have suddenly exposed such a lie in order to live? Of course they would have. If you were facing death, wouldn't you expose a lie to save your own life? But not one of the apostles changed their story. Why? Because they could not deny what was true. Christ had risen. He was alive!

The Absence of Reasonable Alternative Explanations

Because the resurrection of Jesus Christ is tantamount to the Christian faith, it's easy to see why people have attempted to explain it away. Throughout time, numerous arguments have arisen against the validity of the Resurrection. Let's examine the most common arguments people give as to why the Resurrection did not take place:

The Swoon Theory

The Premise

One of the most commonly held theories against the Resurrection is the "swoon theory." This theory proposes that Jesus did not rise from the dead at all, because He actually did not die on the cross. Instead, Jesus went into a deep coma or swoon from the severe pain and trauma of the Crucifixion. Then, in the cool atmosphere of the tomb, Christ revived, somehow was able to get out of the strips of cloths that were wrapped tightly upon Him, and then appeared to His disciples.

The Rebuttal

The Roman guards were experts at execution and would be put to death if they allowed a condemned man to escape death. The guards were so certain Jesus was dead, that they did not even bother to break His legs (see John 19:33–37). And when the spear they thrust into Jesus' side brought forth blood and water, they had the final proof of His death, for this occurs when the heart stops beating.

The swoon theory is even less believable when you take into account that Jesus would have had to survive massive blood loss from the scourging, the nail wounds, and the spear thrust from the Roman guard. In addition, Jesus would have had to endure approximately three days without food or drink in His weakened condition. In His emaciated state, Jesus would have to manage to unwrap Himself from His grave clothes (which were glued together hard and fast by the myrrh He was buried with) and then, on His own, roll away the massive stone of the tomb. Finally, He would have had to convince His followers that He had risen from the dead—despite His weakened appearance—and travel countless miles in that condition to make many appearances to His disciples over the next forty days.

This theory, understandably, is rarely promoted today. However, there are still some people who conveniently hang their doubt on this theory.

The No Burial Theory
The Premise
Christ was never put in the tomb to begin with. Instead, He was thrown into a mass grave for criminals, according to Roman custom.

The Rebuttal
If this were true, neither the Jewish leaders nor the Roman soldiers would have bothered to seal the tomb if they knew His body was not inside it (see Matthew 27:62–66). Moreover, to disprove Jesus' resurrection, they simply had to retrieve the body and display it to the world.

The Mass Hallucination Theory
The Premise
Everyone who claimed to see the risen Lord was hallucinating out of an earnest desire to see Jesus alive again.

The Rebuttal

Hallucinations typically occur with people who are in one way or another expecting them. But biblical evidence reveals that Jesus' disciples were not expecting to see Him alive again (see Mark 16:10–11). The Resurrection came as a complete and total shock. Additionally, hallucinations, once started, are continual; but the disciples saw Jesus for a limited time and then they ceased to see Him again. Scripture also records that five hundred people saw Christ on a single occasion (see 1 Corinthians 15:6). It is one matter for one single person to hallucinate, but a completely different thing for five hundred people to have the identical hallucination simultaneously, which is hardly possible.

Blessed Are Those Who Haven't Seen Me and Believe

The Apostle Thomas was skeptical about the Resurrection. He wanted evidence. Eight days after the Resurrection, Christ appeared to Thomas and showed him His nail scars and wounded side. How did Thomas reply? He believed and said, "My Lord and my God" (John 20:28). Some people might argue that it was easy for Thomas to believe. After all, Thomas saw the risen Lord face to face. But we need to keep in mind Jesus' words to Thomas, "because you have seen Me, you have believed. Blessed are those who have not seen and yet have believed." (John 20:29).

The fact of the matter is that belief in Christ is not a case of stacking up the evidence. Many people saw Christ after the Resurrection and still did not believe (for example, see Matthew 28:1–15). Belief in Jesus is founded upon faith. You might say, "Show me and I will believe." For all practical purposes, God says, "Believe and I will show you." Just take a step of faith. All of your questions won't necessarily be answered when you first come to Christ. When I first made my commitment to follow Jesus Christ, I still had questions, problems, and sins that needed to be dealt with. But with as much faith as I had, I took that little step. God more than met me halfway. He will do the same for you.

THE APPEARANCES OF THE RISEN CHRIST

To help unfold the events between Christ's resurrection and ascension, below is a chronology of the ten appearances of the risen Christ as recorded in Scripture.

SUMMARY OF EVENTS	THE PLACE
Christ appears to Mary Magdalene and commissions her to tell the disciples about His soon-coming ascension.	The Garden Tomb
On their way to tell the disciples about the Resurrection, Jesus appears to the women and commands them to tell the disciples to go to Galilee.	A Road Near Jerusalem
Cleopas and another disciple encounter Christ without recognizing Him. When they realize it is Jesus, they go and tell the others.	The Road to Emmaus
Cleopas and the other disciple arrive in Jerusalem and are greeted with the news that Christ appeared to the Apostle Peter.	Unknown
Christ appears to Cleopas and the other disciples, eats with them, teaches them the Scriptures, and tells them to preach to all the nations.	Behind Locked Doors
Christ shows Himself to Thomas and the other disciples, providing Thomas the opportunity to see His wounds and believe in Him.	Behind Locked Doors
Peter, Thomas, Nathanael, John, James, and two other disciples see Jesus while fishing. There Christ challenges Peter and says, "Follow me."	The Sea of Galilee
Christ meets the eleven disciples, and perhaps hundreds of others (see 1 Corinthians 15:6), and gives them the Great Commission.	An Unnamed Mountain
Christ appears to the eleven disciples as they are eating, rebukes them, and commands them to preach the Good News to everyone.	Unknown
Christ leads the eleven disciples to Bethany on the Mount of Olives, promises them the Holy Spirit, and ascends into heaven.	The Mount of Olives

THE TIME	THE SCRIPTURE
Early Easter Morning, While It Was Still Dark	John 20:11–18
Early Easter Morning	Matthew 28:5–15. See also Mark 16:2–8; Luke 24:1–11
Easter around Noon	Mark 16:12–13; Luke 24:13–35
Easter Day	Luke 24:34; 1 Corinthians 15:5
Easter Evening	Luke 24:35–49; John 20:19–23
Eight Days after Easter	John 20:24–29
At Dawn, between Easter and the Ascension	John 21:1–25
Between Easter and the Ascension	Matthew 28:16–20
Between Easter and the Ascension	Mark 16:14–18
Forty Days after Easter	Luke 24:50–53; Acts 1:4–11

"GO therefore and make **DISCIPLES** of All Nations..." MATTHEW 28:19

CHAPTER 8

THE GREAT COMMISSION AND THE BIRTH OF THE CHURCH

"Jesus wants today's church to have a profound impact on its culture, to turn the world upside down for Him."

Conversion Is the Work of God

I once heard a story about a time when Billy Graham was traveling by plane. There was a very inebriated man on the flight who heard that the famed evangelist was on board. Eager to meet Dr. Graham, the gentleman got up out of his seat and with a slurred voice announced, "I want to meet Billy Graham!" One of the flight attendants attempted to control the situation by telling him, "Sir, you have to take your seat." But the man still insisted, "I want to meet Billy Graham!" As his voice grew louder, Billy overheard the commotion, got up out of his seat, and stepped into the aisle to greet the gentleman. The man fiercely shook his hand and boasted, "Billy Graham, you don't know how much your preaching has helped me." Billy thought to himself, *It couldn't have helped him too much.*

There are countless people today who will profess faith in Christ, but do not reflect it in their lifestyle. Conversion is the work of God, but throughout Scripture, He has used human instruments to bring about the salvation of the lost. The fact of the matter is that God uses willing Christians to perform His will.

I recently read an alarming statistic that ninety-five percent of all Christians have never led another person to Jesus Christ. It is interesting to wonder if this is because Christians are out there trying and haven't had the blessing of seeing someone come to Christ? Or is it because few of us are trying and many of us have never even spoken up? Sadly, I think it is the latter of the two. Granted, God is the only One who can bring about the conversion of a person. I can't do it. You can't do it. Only God can. But somehow He involves us in the process.

This is why we all need to ask ourselves whether or not we have done our part. Have we made ourselves available to the work of evangelism? Have we even planted that seed or at least made an attempt?

The Great Commission
I know that for some the idea of evangelism can seem daunting and overwhelming. But as we come to the Scriptures, we will see that God has provided us with the authority and power to reach this lost world—one person at a time. Before Christ ascended into heaven, Jesus told His disciples how. Let's read about it in Matthew 28:18–20:

> Jesus came and spoke to them, saying, "All authority has been given to Me in heaven and on earth. Go therefore and make disciples of all the nations, baptizing them in the name of the Father and of the Son and of the Holy Spirit, teaching them to observe all things that I have commanded you; and lo, I am with you always, even to the end of the age."

There are two very important things to consider in this statement of our Lord. First, in the original language it is a command. That is why we refer to this statement of the Lord as the Great Commission and not the "great suggestion." It was not a suggestion of Jesus that we carry the gospel into all nations. It was and is a command.

Secondly, these words were not merely directed to the original Eleven. They were given to all followers of the Lord. Sometimes we may think that evangelism should be left to the so called professionals—the pastors, the evangelists, preachers, and missionaries. You may think, "I am not really called to be an evangelist." That may be true, but every believer is called to evangelize.

Unfortunately, instead of fulfilling the Great Commission, some of us are guilty of the "great omission." As followers of Christ, we need to recognize that Scripture teaches that there are sins of commission and omission. A sin of commission involves doing what you should not do. A sin of omission is not doing what you should do. We might pride ourselves on the fact that we have not broken certain commandments or have not done certain things that Scripture forbids. But we are failing to realize that not sharing the gospel can also be a sin. It is a sin of omission. The Bible says, "Therefore, to him who knows to do good and does not do it, to him it is sin" (James 4:17). Our Lord has commanded us to go and share the gospel message with the lost. But how? How do we obtain the power and courage to share God's love with this world? The answer is through Christ.

Be a Disciple Maker

Jesus said, "Go *therefore* and make disciples of all the nations" (Matthew 28:19, emphasis added). Whenever you see the word *therefore*, find out what it is there for. It is drawing upon what has previously been said. What did Jesus say prior to this? He said to the disciples, "All authority has been given to Me in heaven and on earth" (Matthew 28:18). Jesus was making a connection. The connection is that all the power in all of the world and the universe is in Christ. He is over all things. Now consider this: His Spirit lives in you. In other words, He will give you the power to achieve what He has called you to do. God's calling is also His enabling. Sharing God's love is not for you to live out in your own strength. He is going to accomplish it through you as you yield to the Holy Spirit. Therefore, go and preach the gospel. For the sake of those who don't know Christ, go *therefore* and make disciples.

What does it mean to make disciples? Jesus defined it in verse 20, "teaching them to observe all things that I have commanded you." To make disciples of all the nations means to teach people to observe what Jesus commanded. It is to live our faith in this world and to share it with others, teaching it by word and modeling it by example. This concept of making disciples is the willing action of trying to win people to the Lord and then get them up on their feet spiritually. The Apostle Paul substantiated this when he wrote, "Him we preach, warning every man and teaching every man in all wisdom, that we may present every man perfect in Christ Jesus" (Colossians 1:28). This is what we need to do—help people come to faith and help them grow in their faith spiritually. This is the Great Commission.

But the knowledge of Christ's commission sets a choice before us. We can evangelize or we can fossilize. If you are only taking in the truth of God and don't have an outlet for that truth, you can begin to stagnate spiritually. If you know someone who is young in the faith and is discovering these things for the first time, it can reinvigorate and even bring personal, spiritual revival to your own life.

You may think you do not know enough to share your faith with another person. I suggest you know a lot more than you may realize. The average Christian has a lot of embedded truth that has never been utilized. And if you don't feel as though you know what you need to know, equip yourself. For the Bible says "Set apart Christ as Lord. Always be prepared to give an answer to everyone who asks you to give the reason for the hope that you have. But do this with gentleness and respect" (1 Peter 3:15 NIV). I would also encourage you to get a copy of the *Start! Bible*. I had the privilege of writing the notes for this Bible, and as you carefully study what is there, you will better equip yourself to the task of effectively sharing the gospel message.

The Harvest Is Great

Today, ask yourself, *When was the last time I initiated a conversation about my faith?* We all need to put up our little spiritual antennas and pray, "Lord, I'm available. Call on me today. Use me." Those opportunities are out there. You only have to be willing, and the Lord will use you to make disciples.

Before Jesus died and rose again, He told His disciples, "The harvest truly is plentiful, but the laborers are few. Therefore pray the Lord of the harvest to send out laborers into His harvest" (Matthew 9:37–38). We, as believers, are God's workers. God has chosen to work through human instruments. He has chosen to use people just like you and just like me. You are someone God wants to work through, and indeed can use, to bring the life-changing message of the gospel to this generation. Will you be open? Will you be available? The opportunities are there. But it is up to you to seize them.

The True Source of Our Strength

One night, a number of years ago, hurricane winds battered an American town. In the morning, people emerged from their homes and shelters to assess the damage. The power of the storm quickly became apparent to one investigator, who was baffled by an amazing discovery. Imbedded in a telephone pole, he found a flimsy, plastic drinking straw. Obviously, under normal circumstances, a straw could never penetrate a telephone pole. The tremendous power of the wind is what drove that straw like a spike into the wood.

Christians are similar to that drinking straw. Apart from the power of the Holy Spirit, we could never impact our world for Christ. It is the power of the Holy Spirit that enables us to love our neighbor, forgive one another, and preach the Good News. This is why Jesus Christ left the disciples. He left so He could send the Holy Spirit to empower all believers.

During the forty days between the Resurrection and the Ascension, Christ appeared to His disciples a number of times. He was there for His followers to reach out and touch. Can you imagine being one of those believers who walked and talked with the Lord? The first-century believers could hear Christ's voice with their own ears and see Him with their own eyes.

But the disciples were still confused about Christ's purpose for the world even with the risen Lord before their very eyes. They thought He was going to free Israel from Roman rule and restore their kingdom (see Acts 1:6). But what occurred forty days after the Resurrection amazed Christ's disciples. Instead of overturning the Roman government, Jesus led the disciples up to the Mount of Olives, blessed them, and ascended into heaven. Two angels then appeared afterward and signaled to them that this was the last time Christ would appear to them in this fashion. The angels asked the disciples, "Men of Galilee, why do you stand gazing up into heaven? This same Jesus, who was taken up from you into heaven, will so come in like manner as you saw Him go into heaven" (Acts 1:11). The angels revealed to the disciples that their Lord was now in heaven sitting at His exalted place at the right hand of God. There He would rule until He returned again at the Second Coming. Jesus' purpose was spiritual, while the disciples' purpose was political.

You Will Receive Power

Jesus, however, did not leave His disciples without direction. Just before He ascended into heaven, He reminded them of the promise concerning the Holy Spirit. There on the Mount of Olives, He proclaimed, "But you shall receive power when the Holy Spirit has come upon you; and you shall be witnesses to Me in Jerusalem, and in all Judea and Samaria, and to the end of the earth" (Acts 1:8). That promise was fulfilled on the day of Pentecost. Seven weeks after the Resurrection, the Holy Spirit came upon the disciples and transformed their lives. The coming of the Holy Spirit impacted their lives to the point that they could not keep it to themselves. As Peter and John said, "For we cannot but speak the things which we have seen and heard" (Acts 4:20).

This power that the first-century Christians experienced is also available to believers today. The Holy Spirit comes to live in every person who has put their faith in Christ. The Holy Spirit seals us. He dwells in us. But there is a dimension of this power promised that will better enable us, as Christ's followers, to be witnesses for Him. Every Christian needs this power to be the person God has called them to be. It's a supernatural courage to stand up and be counted. And God can give you this boldness today.

The early church was completely dependent upon the work of the Holy Spirit. They were dependent upon God using them. They didn't have many of the advantages that we have today, if you even want to call them that. They didn't have technology like printing presses, radio, television, and the Internet. But the early church possessed the power of God's Spirit in their lives.

Occasionally when we think of the power of the Spirit, we get a little concerned. We all have seen abuses in this area by some people who engage in unusual and sometimes flat out bizarre behavior that they attribute to the Holy Spirit. But I want you to know that God doesn't provide His power for us merely to have an emotional experience. He doesn't give us that power just so we can feel good about ourselves or simply have a wonderful time at church. It's a practical power to go out and impact this world that we are living in.

I think we need to ask for this power in our lives. I think every one of us should pray for God to fill us with His Spirit today. For some of us it will be the first time we have ever received this dimension of power to be a witness for Jesus Christ. For others, we need a refill. Did you know God likes to give refills? For instance, when you run out of gas, you don't say, "Time to get rid of the car. It ran out of gas." No, when the car is out of gas, that simply means it's time to get a refill. In the same way, the Bible tells us in Ephesians 5:18, "Be filled with the Spirit." In the original language that could be better translated "Be constantly filled with the Holy Spirit." The Holy Spirit is Someone we need in our lives.

Through the Holy Spirit, the early believers—the church—began to turn their world upside down. They challenged the rulers of their land, preached in uncharted territory, and many even died for their faith—all empowered by God's Spirit. Indeed, that is what Jesus wants the church—the collective body of Christian believers—to do. Like that small group of first-century Christians, Jesus wants today's church to have a profound impact on its culture, to turn the world upside down for Him (see Acts 17:6). It is possible—if we do it in God's way and in God's power.

God's Purpose for the Church

As believers empowered by the Holy Spirit and members of the body of Christ, God has a purpose for us. We need to be aware of God's will and desire for His church. In other words, is the church's primary purpose to help meet the needs of you and your family? Is it here to win the world for Christ? Does it exist to right the world of social wrongs? Or is it a hospital for saints and sinners? You might be surprised by the Bible's answer. None of these suggestions alone is the reason the church exists.

I believe the church is on this earth for three reasons:
1. Exalt God
2. Edify believers
3. Evangelize the lost

Another way to put it is,
1. Upward (Exaltation)
2. Inward (Edification)
3. Outward (Evangelization)

The first purpose of the church is to exalt God. This is the Christian's upward focus in life. God put us on this earth to know Him and to glorify Him (see Ephesians 1:12). That idea may come as a revelation to some people. Many people think they are on this earth to make their mark on society, or they may think their purpose is to go out and merely find a career and become successful. Others feel their reason for living is to have a family or find personal happiness. But the Bible teaches that we are put on this earth primarily to know and bring glory to the God who created us. Peter pointed this purpose out when he wrote, "But you are a chosen generation, a royal priesthood, a holy nation, His own special people, that you may proclaim the praises of Him who called you out of darkness into His marvelous light" (1 Peter 2:9). As you can see, the Bible is clear that the church exists to exalt and praise God. First and foremost, our relationships should be focused upward.

The second function of the church is to concentrate inward. This means the church is to edify other believers in the body of Christ. The Apostle Paul said that his goal was not merely to evangelize, but to warn believers, teach them with all the wisdom of God, and present them to God, perfect in their relationship to Christ (see Colossians 1:28). That is why we are here. That is what church is about. The church doesn't exist just to sing a few songs, teach a message, and give an offering. We are here to be equipped and equip one another. Only as mature, Spirit-filled believers, can we have the maximum impact on the world for God's glory.

Lastly, God has called the church to go outward. In other words, we are to go into all the world and evangelize the lost. This purpose is a natural outgrowth of the first two. If we are exalting God and edifying one another, we will naturally want to share the hope of salvation with others through our loving actions and words. We also will want to obey the Lord. Healthy sheep will reproduce themselves. This was Christ's commandment before He ascended into heaven: "Go into all the world and preach the gospel to every creature" (Mark 16:15). The church should do just that.

It is essential that we keep these principles in their proper balance. The church is not to emphasize one principle at the expense of the other or take them out of their proper order. The church has to have balance. It needs to exalt God; it needs to edify the believers;

and it needs to evangelize the lost. All of these principles must be emphasized on a regular basis to keep the church strong and healthy.

Turning the World Upside Down

Maintaining the proper balance of the church would be impossible on our own strength. But on the Day of Pentecost, God provided believers in Christ with the strength to do so through the Holy Spirit. We can't do it on our own, but by being energized and empowered by the Holy Spirit we can do all things through the strength of Jesus Christ (see Philippians 4:13). That's why we need to say, "Lord, there is no way we can impact our culture in our own strength. We can't do it through programs. We can't do it through gimmicks. We can't do it through any of our own devices. We need a power beyond ourselves. We need to be like that little straw thrust into a telephone pole by the power of a hurricane. Lord, we are flimsy. We are weak. We can't do it on our own. But with your power launching us into this culture, we can make a difference. We need You in our lives."

It is my prayer that we—the church—will pray for the Holy Spirit to bring power into our lives so that we might turn our world upside down for the Lord.

HOW TO HAVE A RELATIONSHIP WITH JESUS CHRIST

If you desire to have a relationship with Christ or if you want to lead a friend or a family member to Christ, I want to share with you a few simple things you need to know:

First, realize that you are a sinner.

No matter how good a life we try to live, we still will fall miserably short of God's standards. The Bible says, "There is none righteous, no, not one" (Romans 3:10). The word *righteous* means "one who is as he or she ought to be." Apart from Jesus Christ, we cannot become the people we "ought to be."

Second, recognize that Jesus Christ died on the cross for you.

Scripture says, "But God demonstrates His own love toward us, in that while we were still sinners, Christ died for us" (Romans 5:8). God gave His very Son to die in our place when we least deserved it. As the Apostle Paul said, "[Christ] loved me and gave Himself for me" (Galatians 2:20).

Third, repent of your sin.

The Bible tells us to repent and be converted (see Acts 3:19). The word *repent* means to change our direction in life. Instead of running from God, we can run toward Him.

Fourth, receive Jesus Christ into your life.

Becoming a Christian is not merely believing some creed or going to church on Sunday. It is having Christ Himself take residence in your life and heart. Jesus said, "Behold, I stand at the door and knock. If anyone hears My voice and opens the door, I will come in …" (Revelation 3:20). Jesus stands at the door of your life right now and is knocking. He says that if you will hear His voice and open the door, He will come in.

If you would like to know that when you die, you will go to heaven, and if you want to have a life that is full of purpose and meaning, then pray this suggested prayer and mean it with your heart:

Dear Lord Jesus, I know I am a sinner. I believe You died for my sins and rose again from the dead. Right now, I turn from my sins and open the door of my heart and life. I confess You as my personal Lord and Savior. Thank you for saving me. Amen.

If you prayed that prayer, I encourage you to learn more about what it means to follow Christ. To help you with this, you can receive spiritual resources from Harvest Ministries by writing to us or by registering your decision at **www.harvest.org/knowgod.**

HARVEST MINISTRIES
P.O. Box 4000
Riverside, CA 92514

www.harvest.org